52
Lessons
for
Christianpreneurs

Tasha (TC) Cooper

UpwardAction Media
Washington, DC

Dear Renee

Blessings on

your journey!

Much [♡] TC [?]

52 Lessons for Christianpreneurs by Tasha "TC" Cooper

This book is available at quantity discounts for bulk purchases. For information email **Books@UpwardAction.com** or call (800) 753-6576.

Formatting done by S.W. Cannon of Nonnac Content & Press
https://sw-cannon.selz.com/categories/book-services

ISBN: **978-0-9912536-0-9 (P)**
ISBN: **978-0-9912536-1-6 (E)**

This book is dedicated to my front row:

Catheia E. Greene for believing in me and always supporting my crazy ideas. I know you are watching all of this unfold from your seat in heaven. I miss you.

Nan for providing me with a firm foundation in Christ that has guided my entire life. I can hardly believe that you left us so suddenly. I think about you all the time. I know you are up in heaven with Gramps, Aunt Theia and all of your sisters and brothers cheering and supporting, just like you have always done.

Mommy and Daddy for always supporting me, even when you think I am being impractical. ☺ I love you!

Mischa and Nora, it is my dream that my Christian-based business makes it possible for you girls to chase whatever dreams you have without any fear of failure and without being concerned by what is reasonable or practical. I love you both!

Dr. Sonya for being the best sister-cousin in the universe and helping to convince folks that my ideas are not so crazy ☺. Your support means everything.

Aunt Betty for encouraging me through tough times and being my personal cheerleader! I love and appreciate you so much.

Marenda for being my best friend in life and business. We have come a long way since Hampton University. You are truly my Queen of Inspiration. Your journey inspires me.

CONNECT WITH TC ON SOCIAL MEDIA

Facebook:	http://Facebook.com/UpwardAction
Twitter:	http://Twitter.com/UpwardAction
Instagram:	http://Instagram.com/UpwardAction
Periscope:	http://Periscope.TV/UpwardAction

BOOK TC FOR SPEAKING ENGAGEMENTS

Upward Action LLC
www.UpwardAction.com
Books@UpwardAction.com
(800) 753-6576

FREE AUDIO RECORDINGS

Receive free audio recordings for the first 15 lessons in this book by going to www.Christianpreneurs.net/audio. We'll deliver an audio lesson to your email inbox every week for 15 weeks.

The complete audio program is valued at $27.00. This is our special thank you for purchasing 52 Lessons for Christianpreneurs: Faith. Focus. Flow.

DOWNLOAD YOUR FREE
"HOW TO READ THIS BOOK" GUIDE

Download the free reading guide *"How To Read 52 Lessons for Christianpreneurs: Faith. Focus Flow."* at www.Christianpreneurs.net/guide.

This reading companion provides step-by-step instructions for exactly how to get the most value from this book. It's perfect for individual study, accountability partners and book clubs.

Upward**Action**₍₍c

At UpwardAction® we help clients like you create, curate and communicate compelling digital content that gets results.

When you are ready to make your digital content work for you, let's talk!

SERVICES:

- Social Media Strategy
- LinkedIn Consulting
- Facebook Advertising
- LinkedIn Advertising
- Twitter Advertising

Contact Us:

Email:	WeCare@UpwardAction.com
Skype:	TC Cooper @ UpwardAction
Telephone:	(800) 753-6576
Website:	www.UpwardAction.com

Social Media Audit

The UpwardAction® social media audit includes a comprehensive review of the social media sites your company or law firm is using and specific recommendations for how to increase engagement and profitability. If you are not currently using any social network, our experts will tell you exactly how to get started with the best social network for your business objectives. Our recommendations will be based on both your corporate goals and your available resources.

Testimonial: Folks look at me as a social media expert but it was actually TC Cooper who showed me how to automate my daily posts. You need to hire her before your competition does!

Andrew Morrison, *Small Business Camp*

Contact Us:

Email:	WeCare@UpwardAction.com
Skype:	TC Cooper @ UpwardAction
Telephone:	(800) 753-6576
Website:	www.UpwardAction.com

READ THIS FIRST

The Bible provides specific instructions for how to live purposeful, empowered lives and how to build successful businesses. It is filled with knowledge and wisdom that will assist you in creating, maintaining and growing a lucrative business that is a blessing to many. While sometimes written in parables or hidden in historical text, the truths in the Bible are profound and will produce consistent results when acted upon in faith. Many of these Biblical lessons are repeated over and over again throughout the Bible, but in different ways, to ensure that you understand the lessons being taught.

This book follows the blueprint of repetition created by the Bible in that you will find similar lessons throughout the book as these lessons appear in different Bible verses. The importance of creating goals and taking actions that are specific, measurable, actionable, relevant and time-bound (**S.M.A.R.T.**) are two messages that are often repeated. I use the S.M.A.R.T. acronym throughout this book in both lessons and affirmations. Other repeated messages include: the importance of diligence, the necessity of hiring wise counsel, and the power of having an unshakable **will** to **win**.

While reading the lessons included in these pages, keep in mind that God's plan for your life reigns supreme. In the places where I encourage you to pray and ask God for guidance, please do so. Ask God to align your will with His will, because when the two are in alignment, you will experience the success and joy that are referenced in the Bible and throughout this book. When your will and God's will are out of alignment, lasting success will be elusive.

Also keep in mind that your life is not just for you. Your life and your experiences belong to God and are sometimes used by God to be a blessing to someone else. Be encouraged – regardless of what is happening in your life and your business. Rest assured that no part of your journey as a Christianpreneur is wasted.

In fact, you are a living testimony for the power, grace and mercy of our Lord and Savior – Jesus Christ.

As you read this book, you will see that I capitalize the word "Work." Every time you see this word capitalized, know that I am writing about the actions you must take in order to make the vision that God has given you a reality. Your God-inspired actions make up your "Work."

It is my hope and prayer that you will read and implement at least one lesson from this book and complete the accompanying S.M.A.R.T. goal exercise every week for the next 52 weeks. A large version of the S.M.A.R.T. goals chart can be found on the last page of this book. Feel free to make copies of this graphic and use in your weekly goal planning. Be sure to also download my detailed guide for getting the most value from this book at www.Christianpreneurs.net/guide.

I encourage you to periodically go back and review the prayers you have written, signed and dated for each lesson that you have completed. Do this from time to time and you will be blown way from seeing just how much God is moving in your life in both the little things and big things that your heart desires.

If you are diligent about meditating on the Bible-based truths contained in the lessons and affirmations written in these pages and also taking S.M.A.R.T. action, your business will flourish and your life will be transformed. Give it a try!

Love & Light!
Tasha "TC" Cooper

TABLE OF LESSONS

TABLE OF LESSONS

A MESSAGE FROM TC TO YOU!

Welcome to the first edition of my book – *52 Lessons for Christianpreneurs: Faith. Focus. Flow.* I pray that you receive the lessons I share in this book with the same spirit of love in which I have written them for you. If this book has an impact on your life or business, I would love to read about it. Email me at **52Lessons@UpwardAction.com.** If you have a Twitter account, you can also Tweet me at **www.Twitter.com/UpwardAction.**

I look forward to reading your stories!
~TC

LESSON 1

JUST DO IT

Careful planning puts you ahead in the long run;
hurry and scurry puts you further behind.

Proverbs 21:5 (The Message)

Sustainable success does not come from luck or chance; it happens by design. The Bible says careful planning puts you ahead in the long run. The Bible also makes it clear that the lack of planning leads to hurry and scurry. Both will waste your time, reduce the chances you will accomplish your goals, and could destroy your dream of building a profitable and sustainable Christ-centered business.

"Hurry-and-scurry" in modern language means to cut corners or take shortcuts. Taking short cuts often leads to leaving out important and necessary steps for sustainable success in order to meet deadlines. Do not let this happen to you.

Proper planning is only a part of what it takes to be successful. Planning means nothing without implementation *(aka "action")*. Once you have developed your plan, take the action necessary to bring your plan to life.

Just as faith without works is dead, plans without strategic action are useless.

Plan carefully.
Do not cut corners.
Take fast action.

Dear Lord,

I give you all honor, glory and praise for blessing me with life and the desire to build a business that serves you. Please help me be diligent in creating **S.M.A.R.T.** plans for my business that will help me to serve more people while building wealth. As I look forward to a new week, I also ask…

That you guide me to my purpose. 7/10/19

Thank you for entrusting me with your Work.

Name   7/10/19 _Date_

Lesson 1 Affirmation

My daily actions are making my goals a reality.

My S.M.A.R.T. Goals for the Week Beginning:				
SPECIFIC	**M**EASURABLE	**A**CTIONABLE	**R**ELEVANT	**T**IME-BOUND
This week I will: *<< insert goal >>*	I know that this goal has been accomplished when: *<insert description>*	I must take the following actions to make this goal a reality: 1. 2. 3.	Accomplishing this goal brings me closer to my vision of: *<insert short description of your vision>*	I will accomplish this goal by: *<insert day, date and time.>* *This date should be within the next 7 days.*

LESSON 2

WORK IN THE PROPER SEASON

Go to the ant, you sluggard;
Consider its ways and be wise!
It has no commander,
No overseer or ruler,
Yet it stores its provisions in summer,
And gathers its food at harvest.

How long will you lay there, you sluggard?
When will you get up from your sleep?

A little sleep, a little slumber,
A little folding of the hands to rest-
And poverty will come on you like a thief
and scarcity like an armed man.

Proverbs 6:6-11 (NIV)

Business owners enjoy great freedom but also have tremendous responsibilities. As a Christianpreneur, you (*and you alone*) are responsible for building and operating a business that creates tremendous value for its clients and customers, meets deadlines, operates within a budget and brings you joy.

Be productive like the ant. Reject procrastination and avoid distractions. If you get off course, pause – do what is necessary to get back on track and start again. If you need support to help you be accountable to yourself and your business, get help. Here's how: find a mastermind group (*create one if you have to*), hire wise counsel or find mentors.

Whatever you do, do something. If you allow yourself to be distracted or deterred from diligently doing what is necessary to grow your business, you will soon find yourself out of business.

Once you have done the mission critical Work that makes your business run smoothly, make time to rest. It is important to embrace the fact that Work is not the only critical ingredient for success; proper rest is equally important.

Sustainable success requires the self-discipline to know when it is time to do the Work of your business and when to take a break for self-care and family. In fact, work/life integration is key to building a business that is good for your bank account and a blessing to your soul. **Make it a part of your life.**

Dear Lord,

I give you all honor, glory and praise for blessing me with life and the desire to build a business that serves you. Please help me focus on the key actions that I must accomplish to move my business forward. When I am tempted to procrastinate, please send a reminder that my diligence is key to my success. As I look forward to a new week, I also ask...

Thank you for entrusting me with your Work.

_____   _____
Name   *Date*

Lesson 2 Affirmation

I am productive and success flows in all areas of my life.

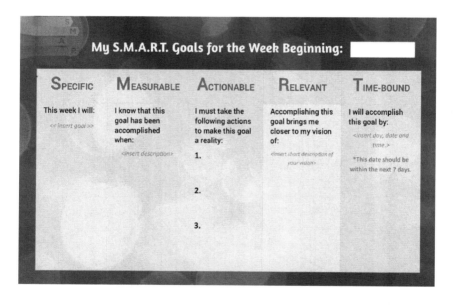

My S.M.A.R.T. Goals for the Week Beginning: _____

SPECIFIC	**M**EASURABLE	**A**CTIONABLE	**R**ELEVANT	**T**IME-BOUND
This week I will: *<< insert goal >>*	I know that this goal has been accomplished when: *<insert description>*	I must take the following actions to make this goal a reality: 1. 2. 3.	Accomplishing this goal brings me closer to my vision of: *<insert short description of your vision>*	I will accomplish this goal by: *<insert day, date and time.>* *This date should be within the next 7 days.

LESSON 3

BE CHEERFUL

Be cheerful no matter what;
Pray all the time;
Thank God no matter what happens.
This is the way God wants you who belong to
Jesus Christ to live.

1 Thessalonians 5:16-18 (The Message)

The journey of entrepreneurship is filled with tremendous highs and devastating lows. To win in life and in business, you must praise God without regard to your circumstances. Know that every low makes you stronger and every high allows you to glorify God and serve more people.

If you want to experience peace of mind throughout your business-building journey, hold on to your faith. Faith is like a muscle, the more you use it – the stronger it becomes. Focus your mind and your actions on manifesting the vision God has placed in your heart. Your focus will lead to your success.

Condition your heart, mind and spirit to be cheerful and thankful throughout your day. This is how God wants you to live!

You will find it easy to focus on the positive when you trust and believe that what awaits you is far greater than what you are experiencing in this moment.

When you approach each day with a strong work ethic and a cheerful spirit, at God's appointed time you will find the success you seek.

Be patient.
Have faith.
Trust God.

Dear Lord,

I give you all honor, glory and praise for blessing me with life and the desire to build a business that serves you. Thank you for your grace and mercy during all of the twists and turns of my life and business. I know that because of your love, all things are working for my good. As I look forward to a new week, I also ask...

Thank you for entrusting me with your Work.

_____   _____
Name   *Date*

Lesson 3 Affirmation

My experiences are leading me to the life and business of my dreams.

My S.M.A.R.T. Goals for the Week Beginning:

SPECIFIC	MEASURABLE	ACTIONABLE	RELEVANT	TIME-BOUND
This week I will: *<< insert goal >>*	I know that this goal has been accomplished when: *<insert description>*	I must take the following actions to make this goal a reality: 1. 2. 3.	Accomplishing this goal brings me closer to my vision of: *<insert short description of your vision>*	I will accomplish this goal by: *<insert day, date and time.>* *This date should be within the next 7 days.

LESSON 4

DISCIPLINE IS LOVE

No discipline seems pleasant at the time, but painful.
Later on, however, it produces a harvest of righteousness
and peace for those who have been trained by it.

Hebrews 12:11 (NIV)

Sometimes we make bad decisions and have to suffer through tough consequences. This is true in business and in life. Thanks to the grace and mercy of our Lord and Savior, Jesus Christ, the consequences you suffer from making bad choices can be used by God to provide you with the training and discipline needed to build a business that honors God, serves people and creates wealth.

Although painful, working your way through the consequences of your decisions builds character. Therefore, do not be discouraged by the bumps and setbacks that result from yesterday. Rest assured that when you trust God and do the Work necessary to bounce back from your past – the lessons learned and discipline developed will prepare you for blessings that are beyond your most incredible dreams.

Dear Lord,

I give you all honor, glory and praise for blessing me with life and the desire to build a business that serves you. Please bless me with the wisdom and discernment that I need to transform every "mistake" or "misstep" that I may make into a learning opportunity. As I look forward to a new week, I also ask…

Thank you for entrusting me with your Work.

_____   _____

Name   *Date*

Lesson 4 Affirmation

I live a disciplined life that gives me
strength and makes me wise.

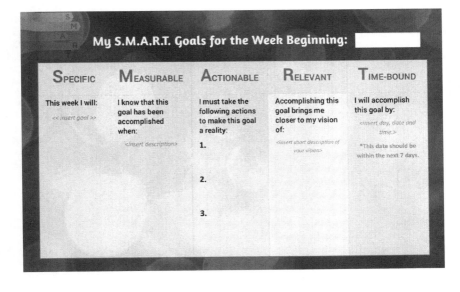

LESSON 5

RUN TO WIN

**You have all been to the stadium
and seen athletes race.
Everyone runs; one wins.
Run to win.**

1 Corinthians 9:24 (The Message)

Building the business of your dreams requires massive levels of faith, focus and commitment. If you want to be a Christianpreneur who has a world-class business that is positioned to win, follow the plans of a world-class athlete who is training to win.

When you procrastinate instead of taking the actions you know are necessary to move your business forward, you are not "running to win." Worse yet, you are wasting your time, talent and the opportunity to be a blessing to your ideal clients and target audience. You are also wasting the opportunity to be a vessel through which God can show his power. God does this through the blessing of Work. If you want God to bless your Work, you have got to give God some Work to bless. ☺

Are you ready to win? Determine what daily actions will lead to success, then accomplish those actions every single day – rain or shine, rested or tired.

**Train to win.
Expect to win.
Celebrate your win.
Start today.**

Dear Lord,

I give you all honor, glory and praise for blessing me with life and the desire to build a business that serves you. Please give me the strength and focus that I need to study my industry and develop creative, yet practical, ideas that position my business to win. As I look forward to a new week, I also ask…

Thank you for entrusting me with your Work.

_____   _____
Name   *Date*

Lesson 5 Affirmation

I am a world-class Christianpreneur
and I am running to win.

My S.M.A.R.T. Goals for the Week Beginning:				
SPECIFIC	**M**EASURABLE	**A**CTIONABLE	**R**ELEVANT	**T**IME-BOUND
This week I will: *<< insert goal >>*	I know that this goal has been accomplished when: *<insert description>*	I must take the following actions to make this goal a reality: 1. 2. 3.	Accomplishing this goal brings me closer to my vision of: *<insert short description of your vision>*	I will accomplish this goal by: *<insert day, date and time.>* *This date should be within the next 7 days.

LESSON 6

TRUST GOD

*Jesus overheard what they were talking about
and said to the leader –
"Don't listen to them. Just trust me."*

Mark 5:36 (The Message)

Ignore the naysayers on your journey to building the business and the life of your dreams. First, trust God. Then, train yourself to become motivated by people who do not believe in you. Be inspired by your "haters" to work harder, be smarter and give more of your best at every single opportunity.

Whenever you feel discouraged or like you are getting off-track, ask God for help. Trust that when you do the Work you have been called to do, the vision God has revealed to you will become a reality.

If you are finding that the people who are most dear to you do not believe that you can accomplish your goals or that your vision will come to pass, remember Romans 3:3-4. Man's unbelief will not nullify God's faithfulness to you. Let every *(unbelieving)* man be a liar but God's word *(to you)* be true.

Don't quit.
Be diligent.
Be patient.
Ignore the chatter around you.
T R U S T God.
Know that your work is never in vain; it will bear fruit.

Dear Lord,

I give you all honor, glory and praise for blessing me with life and the desire to build a business that serves you. Please help me attract godly people into my life who will lift me up with good wishes and encouragement as I ignore the naysayers and trust you. As I look forward to a new week, I also ask...

Thank you for entrusting me with your Work.

_____   _____
Name   *Date*

Lesson 6 Affirmation

My dreams are becoming my reality. I trust God.

My S.M.A.R.T. Goals for the Week Beginning:				
SPECIFIC	**M**EASURABLE	**A**CTIONABLE	**R**ELEVANT	**T**IME-BOUND
This week I will: *<< insert goal >>*	I know that this goal has been accomplished when: *<insert description>*	I must take the following actions to make this goal a reality: 1.	Accomplishing this goal brings me closer to my vision of: *<insert short description of your vision>*	I will accomplish this goal by: *<insert day, date and time >* *This date should be within the next 7 days.*
		2.		
		3.		

35

LESSON 7

DON'T SIT THERE WATCHING

When the clouds are full of water, it rains.
When the wind blows down a tree,
it lies where it falls.
Don't sit there watching the wind.
Do your own work.
Don't stare at the clouds. Get on with your life.

Ecclesiastes 11:3-4 (The Message)

It is easy to sit around lamenting about the past. It is even easier to waste time worrying about everything that could go wrong.

Worry and despair are negative emotions that will not lead to the business and life of your dreams. The more time you waste thinking about your past failures and the failures of others, the further away you will find yourself from achieving your business goals. Stop wasting your time. The past is the past, leave it there.

Do the Work that you have been assigned to do and do it today. Plan the Work that needs to be done tomorrow - make your plans today. Do not procrastinate. Do not delay.

The combination of **s**pecific, **m**easurable, **a**ctionable, **r**elevant and **t**ime-bound (**S.M.A.R.T.**) planning along with rapid implementation will lead to the business of your dreams.

Give it a try.
Start today.

Dear Lord,

I give you all honor, glory and praise for blessing me with life and the desire to build a business that serves you. Help me to stay focused on the Work that must be completed today and follow the plans for tomorrow that I have co-created with you. As I look forward to a new week, I also ask...

Thank you for entrusting me with your Work.

_____   _____
Name   *Date*

Lesson 7 Affirmation

At this very moment I have everything I need to succeed.

SPECIFIC	MEASURABLE	ACTIONABLE	RELEVANT	TIME-BOUND
This week I will: *<< Insert goal >>*	I know that this goal has been accomplished when: *<Insert description>*	I must take the following actions to make this goal a reality: 1. 2. 3.	Accomplishing this goal brings me closer to my vision of: *<Insert short description of your vision>*	I will accomplish this goal by: *<Insert day, date and time.>* *This date should be within the next 7 days.*

My S.M.A.R.T. Goals for the Week Beginning:

LESSON 8

STOP WATCHING THE CLOCK

Go to work in the morning
and stick to it until evening without watching the clock.
You never know
from moment-to- moment
how your work will turn out in the end.

Ecclesiastes 11:6 (The Message)

To build a legacy business, you have got to be so inspired by your vision that you can work around the clock. The passion that inspires your willingness to work without ceasing will give you strength to push past procrastination, distraction, fear and sometimes plain old tiredness. If you want to be successful:

Be ready to work.
Refuse to fail.
Do not quit.

To make God's vision for your life a reality, you must be committed to seeing the vision become a reality - no matter how long it takes or how hard the journey.

Here's why: your very next conversation could lead to an opportunity that alters the course of your life. Your very next article, video, social media update or telephone call could be the thing that changes everything for you.

Whenever you feel tired, discouraged or even defeated, remember the Word of God instructs you to be willing to work around the clock. When you are consistent and diligent in doing the Work that is necessary to build a sustainable business, you will find success right around the corner. This is true no matter how long or short your journey to *"the corner"* seems to be. Keep going. You will get there.

Dear Lord,

I give you all honor, glory and praise for blessing me with life and the desire to build a business that serves you. Please help me focus on doing the Work that I have been called to do without worry or fear that my Work will be in vain. As I look forward to a new week, I also ask…

Thank you for entrusting me with your Work.

_____   _____
Name   *Date*

Lesson 8 Affirmation

I am building wealth and leading others to Christ through my Work.

My S.M.A.R.T. Goals for the Week Beginning:

SPECIFIC	**M**EASURABLE	**A**CTIONABLE	**R**ELEVANT	**T**IME-BOUND
This week I will: *<< insert goal >>*	I know that this goal has been accomplished when: *<insert description>*	I must take the following actions to make this goal a reality: 1.	Accomplishing this goal brings me closer to my vision of: *<insert short description of your vision>*	I will accomplish this goal by: *<insert day, date and time.>* *This date should be within the next 7 days.*
		2.		
		3.		

LESSON 9

SEEK WISE COUNSEL

**Without good direction, people lose their way;
the more wise counsel you follow,
the better your chances.**

Proverbs 11:14 (The Message)

To build the business of your dreams and not lose yourself in the process, you have to have good direction. This is a word from God. Good direction comes from following guidance from the Bible and listening to the advice of wise counsel *(aka "mentors, coaches, experts and consultants")*.

Successful business owners are intentional about surrounding themselves with subject matter experts. All great leaders, athletes and business owners have accelerated their path to success through being coached, taught, inspired or otherwise motivated by wise counsel. The ones who enjoy peace of mind also have a spiritual advisor on their team.

If you think hiring a mentor, coach, consultant or other wise counsel is currently out of your reach, do not stress out or be discouraged. You can be mentored and guided by the advice of someone you consider to be wise counsel without having a direct relationship with that person. If you do not have the resources to hire your ideal "wise counsel" right now, start with that person's books, audio programs, digital programs or even their free content on blogs and social media. This can get you headed in the right direction ... if you are committed to learning and disciplined enough to take action.

When you have more resources, invest in hiring an expert to provide you with the individualized guidance necessary to reach your goals faster. Here's why: if you want to accelerate your journey to success, 1-on-1 support is important. So - stretch yourself, cut expenses and make sacrifices to get the guidance you need.

If you need help using social media to increase your impact, influence and income, contact UpwardAction®. You can learn all about our work and also find our contact information on our website at www.UpwardAction.com. We can help you leverage the power of social marketing to stand out and attract your ideal clients.

Success leaves clues.
Follow them.

Dear Lord,

I give you all honor, glory and praise for blessing me with life and the desire to build a business that serves you. Please lead me to wise counsel to guide me as I complete the Work you have assigned for my life. Help me to be discerning enough to recognize wise counsel when encountered, humble enough to listen to good advice when given and diligent enough take action quickly. As I look forward to a new week, I also ask...

Thank you for entrusting me with your Work.

_____   _____
Name   *Date*

Lesson 9 Affirmation

God leads wise counsel into my life.

My S.M.A.R.T. Goals for the Week Beginning:

SPECIFIC	MEASURABLE	ACTIONABLE	RELEVANT	TIME-BOUND
This week I will: *<< insert goal >>*	I know that this goal has been accomplished when: *<insert description>*	I must take the following actions to make this goal a reality: 1. 2. 3.	Accomplishing this goal brings me closer to my vision of: *<insert short description of your vision>*	I will accomplish this goal by: *<insert day, date and time.>* *This date should be within the next 7 days.

LESSON 10

YOU CAN CREATE WEALTH

**But remember the Lord your God,
for it is he who gives you the ability to produce wealth.**

Deuteronomy 8:18 (NIV)

God is the source of your wealth. Do not ever forget it.

If you are being diligent in your Work, but you are not experiencing the success you know is possible – do not fear, you are in a season of sowing. Do not be discouraged by this season of your life or business; learn from it.

Trust that if you do not quit, God will continue giving you the strength you need to do the Work necessary to produce wealth. Keep working, keep praying, keep sowing - your season of harvest is coming.

If you are in a season of harvest, give thanks to God who has made it possible! While you are celebrating and praising God for your success, continue to plant seeds for your next harvest. This is the cycle of sowing and reaping that leads to legacy success in business and in life.

Dear Lord,

I give you all honor, glory and praise for blessing me with life and the desire to build a business that serves you. Thank you for giving me the ability to create wealth. Help me remember that building wealth is a marathon not a sprint, and I will be successful if I do not quit. As I look forward to a new week, I also ask...

Thank you for entrusting me with your Work.

_____   _____
Name   *Date*

Lesson 10 Affirmation

I am sowing seeds that will produce a harvest in God's time.

My S.M.A.R.T. Goals for the Week Beginning:				
SPECIFIC	**M**EASURABLE	**A**CTIONABLE	**R**ELEVANT	**T**IME-BOUND
This week I will: *<< insert goal >>*	I know that this goal has been accomplished when: *<insert description>*	I must take the following actions to make this goal a reality: 1. 2. 3.	Accomplishing this goal brings me closer to my vision of: *<insert short description of your vision>*	I will accomplish this goal by: *<insert day, date and time.>* **This date should be within the next 7 days.*

LESSON 11

DON'T BE TIMID

**The spirit God gave us does not make us timid,
but gives us power, love and self-discipline.**

2 Timothy 1:7 (NIV)

The idea that has become your business is a gift from God.
The manifestation of that idea into a thriving business is yet
another gift from God. God doesn't want you to be shy with
his gifts. Instead, God wants you to be courageous, loving and
disciplined in sharing your gifts with the world around you.

The Bible tells us that the spirit God gave us does not make us
timid or shy. Therefore, walk in your power by boldly and
confidently telling others about your business and its benefits.
Do this knowing that your business can transform the lives of
those who need your programs, products and services. *If you
do not think that the programs, products and services your
business provides to clients and customers can transform their
lives, you need to rethink your business.*

Transformation can only happen when people know about
your business and how it can help them achieve their goals. In
order for people to know about your business, you have to tell
people about it. Furthermore, if you want your business to
expand, you must put systems in place to automate as much as
reasonable.

If you are ready for your business to soar, follow these steps:

Tell people about your business.
Create systems to streamline your business processes.
Automate as much as possible.

When you are disciplined in doing the Work of your business, you will discover just how disciplined God is in blessing your business. Give it a try. Start this week. If you need help with automate, contact my office. You can get in touch with us by going to www.UpwardAction.com. You have nothing to lose and everything to gain.

Dear Lord,

I give you all honor, glory and praise for blessing me with life and the desire to build a business that serves you. Please help me to do the Work you have called me to do with a sound mind and magnetic spirit that attracts my ideal clients and customers. As I look forward to a new week, I also ask…

Thank you for entrusting me with your Work.

Name	_Date_

Lesson 11 Affirmation

My business is a blessing to my clients and customers.

My S.M.A.R.T. Goals for the Week Beginning: _____

SPECIFIC	MEASURABLE	ACTIONABLE	RELEVANT	TIME-BOUND
This week I will: << insert goal >>	I know that this goal has been accomplished when: <insert description>	I must take the following actions to make this goal a reality: 1. 2. 3.	Accomplishing this goal brings me closer to my vision of: <insert short description of your vision>	I will accomplish this goal by: <insert day, date and time.> *This date should be within the next 7 days.

LESSON 12

BE DILIGENT

Our people must learn to be diligent in their work
so that all necessities are met (especially among
the needy) and they don't end up with
nothing to show for their lives.

Titus 3:14 (The Message)

Diligence is necessary to live a productive life and leave a legacy that serves people now and will continue to serve in the years to come. When you are diligent in doing your Work, your business will not only provide all the necessities of your life, there will be enough overflow to bless others.

The opposite of diligence is procrastination. Success is the result of consistent, timely action - not procrastination. In fact, if you are lazy, undisciplined, and unfocused – your business will suffer, your time will be wasted and you will have nothing to show for the gift that is your life.

Take action.
Start today.

Dear Lord,

I give you all honor, glory and praise for blessing me with life and the desire to build a business that serves you. Please bless me with the strength I need to avoid wasteful activities and the diligence I need to accomplish goals that will move my business forward. As I look forward to a new week, I also ask...

Thank you for entrusting me with your Work.

_____   _____
Name   *Date*

Lesson 12 Affirmation

My life bears fruit that serves the world around me.

My S.M.A.R.T. Goals for the Week Beginning: _____

SPECIFIC	MEASURABLE	ACTIONABLE	RELEVANT	TIME-BOUND
This week I will: *<< insert goal >>*	I know that this goal has been accomplished when: *<insert description>*	I must take the following actions to make this goal a reality: 1.	Accomplishing this goal brings me closer to my vision of: *<insert short description of your vision>*	I will accomplish this goal by: *<insert day, date and time.>* *This date should be within the next 7 days.*
		2.		
		3.		

LESSON 13

PRAY MORE. WORRY LESS.

Don't fret or worry.
Instead of worrying, pray.

Let petitions and praises shape your worries into prayers,
letting God know your concerns.

Before you know it, a sense of God's wholeness,
everything coming together for your good,
will come and settle you down.

It's wonderful what happens
when Christ displaces worry at the center of your life.

Philippians 4:6-7 (The Message)

Building a business is not for the faint of heart. There are a lot of moving parts. The work and discipline required to be successful in business can stress you out and cause you to worry - if you allow it. Don't allow it.

When you are feeling stressed because something is not going your way and you have done all that you can do – you have a choice. You can worry or you can pray.

Prayer cancels worry.
Worry cancels prayer.

I invite you to choose prayer, take the action necessary to be successful, and then let God take control. If you trust Him, God will lead you to success that is more fulfilling than you can imagine. Give it a try.

Dear Lord,

I give you all honor, glory and praise for blessing me with life and the desire to build a business that serves you. Please bless me with the discipline that I need to consistently write out my prayers to you, meditate on my prayers, and then store my written prayers in my Bible or another sacred place. As I look forward to a new week, I also ask…

Thank you for entrusting me with your Work.

_____   _____
Name   *Date*

Lesson 13 Affirmation

Today I release my attachment to worry. I trust God with my dreams and vision for the future.

My S.M.A.R.T. Goals for the Week Beginning:

SPECIFIC	**M**EASURABLE	**A**CTIONABLE	**R**ELEVANT	**T**IME-BOUND
This week I will: <<insert goal >>	I know that this goal has been accomplished when: <insert description>	I must take the following actions to make this goal a reality: 1.	Accomplishing this goal brings me closer to my vision of: <insert short description of your vision>	I will accomplish this goal by: <insert day, date and time.> *This date should be within the next 7 days.
		2.		
		3.		

LESSON 14

GIVE IT AWAY

*God can pour on the blessings in astonishing ways
so that you're ready for anything and everything,
more than just ready to do what needs to be done.*

*The most generous God who gives seed to the farmer
that becomes bread for your meal is more than extravagant
with you. He gives you something you can then give away,
which grows into full-formed lives, robust in God, wealthy in
every way, producing with us great praise to God.*

2 Corinthians 9:8, 11 (The Message)

When you invite God into your Work, your business will shift from good to great, from stunning to breath-taking and from ordinary to extraordinary.

When this shift happens, the Bible says not only are God's blessings more than enough to satisfy your every need, there is enough to give away. Here's why: God intended for you to be a blessing to others while you are a blessing to yourself.

You can be a blessing to those around you in a number of ways: provide exceptional service to your clients by doing the unexpected; share valuable information with your target audience for free as often as you can; create exceptional programs, products and services based on what your ideal clients have told you they want; and, ask your ideal clients to purchase your programs, products and/or services.

When you are a blessing to others, you empower them to, in turn, be a blessing to others. This creates a never-ending flow of positive momentum that can transform the world.

Empower your business to be a blessing to others by practicing excellence at all times. This produces great praise to God.

If you need help creating, curating or connecting content on social networks or your online platforms in a way that is compelling and adds value to your industry, UpwardAction® can help. Visit us at www.UpwardAction.com to learn more about how our team of experts can help you give away outstanding content in a way that attracts your ideal clients and generates new business.

Dear Lord,

I give you all honor, glory and praise for blessing me with life and the desire to build a business that serves you. Please bless me with the courage I need to give my best at all times without fear of failure, ridicule or any other negative outcome. As I look forward to a new week, I also ask…

Thank you for entrusting me with your Work.

_____   _____
Name   *Date*

Lesson 14 Affirmation

My business blesses others and inspires them to be a blessing to others.

My S.M.A.R.T. Goals for the Week Beginning: ☐

Specific	Measurable	Actionable	Relevant	Time-bound
This week I will: *<< insert goal >>*	I know that this goal has been accomplished when: *<insert description>*	I must take the following actions to make this goal a reality: 1.	Accomplishing this goal brings me closer to my vision of: *<insert short description of your vision>*	I will accomplish this goal by: *<insert day, date and time.>* *This date should be within the next 7 days.*
		2.		
		3.		

68

LESSON 15

KEEP YOURSELF FUELED

Don't burn out; keep yourselves fueled and aflame.
Be alert servants of the Master, cheerfully expectant.
Don't quit in hard times; pray all the harder.
Help needy Christians; be inventive in hospitality.

Romans 12:11-13 (The Message)

It is important to keep yourself fueled with positive energy. Do this by constantly reminding yourself of the contribution your Work is making to the lives of the people your business serves and the lives of people who are inspired by your journey of Christianpreneurship.

Be thoughtful, strategic and disciplined when moving in the direction of your dreams. Once your Work is done, take time to replenish your body with rest, your mind with the Word of God, and your spirit with both worship and play. Do not work so hard and for so long that you burn out.

You must not burn out.
The world needs you.

Expect the best when building your business and serving clients. Do not be discouraged when your Work feels hard or you grow weary in doing the things that must be done in order to succeed.

Rest.
Re-focus.
Pray harder.

When you take care of your Work, God will take care of you. Be generous, kind and helpful to the people around you. When you are generous with others, God will return this generosity to you in unexpected ways and at unexpected times. Give it a try. You have nothing to lose and everything to gain.

Dear Lord,

I give you all honor, glory and praise for blessing me with life and the desire to build a business that serves you. Help me to rest not only my body but also my mind so that I am energized and renewed - not tired and burned out. As I look forward to a new week, I also ask...

Thank you for entrusting me with your Work.

_____   _____
Name   *Date*

Lesson 15 Affirmation

I honor God by taking exceptional care of my mind, body and spirit.

My S.M.A.R.T. Goals for the Week Beginning:

SPECIFIC	**M**EASURABLE	**A**CTIONABLE	**R**ELEVANT	**T**IME-BOUND
This week I will: *<< insert goal >>*	I know that this goal has been accomplished when: *<insert description>*	I must take the following actions to make this goal a reality: 1. 2. 3.	Accomplishing this goal brings me closer to my vision of: *<insert short description of your vision>*	I will accomplish this goal by: *<insert day, date and time >* *This date should be within the next 7 days.

LESSON 16

SUCCESS IS COMING

I don't think there is any comparison between the present
hard times and the coming good times.
The created world itself can hardly wait
for what's coming next.

Everything in creation is being more or less held back.
God reins it in until both creation and all the creatures
are ready and can be released at the same
moment into the glorious times ahead.

Romans 8:18-21 (The Message)

If you think business is good now, you are going to be
astounded by what God has in store for your life. Do not get
comfortable; keep going.

If you are struggling - be prayerful and stay focused. Know
that through every experience God is helping you become the
person you need to be in order to walk into your destiny.

God has a plan for your business and your life that will be
revealed exactly when you are ready for it. Being ready
requires you to actively seek the Word of God, sit still long
enough to hear God's voice - and then do what God tells you
to do. Will it always be easy? No. Will it always be worth it?
Absolutely.

The struggle you may be going through now is insignificant when compared to what is in store for you. The success that you are experiencing today is nothing compared to what is to come.

Stay in position.
You are winning!

Dear Lord,

I give you all honor, glory and praise for blessing me with life and the desire to build a business that serves you. Please help me stay focused on what is to come and not be discouraged by the obstacles I encounter along my journey to success. As I look forward to a new week, I also ask...

Thank you for entrusting me with your Work.

_____   _____
Name   *Date*

Lesson 16 Affirmation

I am excited about what God has in store for my life.

My S.M.A.R.T. Goals for the Week Beginning: _____

SPECIFIC	MEASURABLE	ACTIONABLE	RELEVANT	TIME-BOUND
This week I will: *<< insert goal >>*	I know that this goal has been accomplished when: *<insert description>*	I must take the following actions to make this goal a reality: 1.	Accomplishing this goal brings me closer to my vision of: *<insert short description of your vision>*	I will accomplish this goal by: *<insert day, date and time.>* *This date should be within the next 7 days.
		2.		
		3.		

LESSON 17

HERE'S THE SECRET

I know what it is to be in need, and
I know what it is to have plenty.

I have learned the secret of being content
in any and every situation, whether well fed or hungry,
whether living in plenty or in want.

I can do all things through Him who gives me strength.

Philippians 4:12 (NIV)

If you need certainty, do not become a business owner. If you want a regimented schedule, the life of an entrepreneur is not for you.

Business ownership is only for the strong, you must be prepared to handle the highs and lows that will come your way.

Do not concern yourself with the lows.
Do not be consumed by the highs.

Trust that every obstacle contains a lesson, and every struggle will make you stronger – if you let it. Know that even if things are wonderful right now, God is able to make them more amazing than you can imagine.

Keep moving forward. Hold on to your faith. Know that thanks to the grace, mercy and power of God, your life and business are a blessing to the world around you.

Dear Lord,

I give you all honor, glory and praise for blessing me with life and the desire to build a business that serves you. Help me to approach the highs and lows of building a God-centered business with a spirit of peace, gratitude and joy. As I look forward to a new week, I also ask…

Thank you for entrusting me with your Work.

_____   _____
Name   *Date*

Lesson 17 Affirmation

I can do all things through Christ Jesus who gives me strength.

My S.M.A.R.T. Goals for the Week Beginning: _____

SPECIFIC	MEASURABLE	ACTIONABLE	RELEVANT	TIME-BOUND
This week I will: *<< insert goal >>*	I know that this goal has been accomplished when: *<insert description>*	I must take the following actions to make this goal a reality: 1. 2. 3.	Accomplishing this goal brings me closer to my vision of: *<insert short description of your vision>*	I will accomplish this goal by: *<insert day, date and time.>* *This date should be within the next 7 days.*

LESSON 18

DON'T SWEAT THE EVIL

**Don't bother your head with braggarts
or wish you could succeed like the wicked.**

**In no time they'll shrivel like grass clippings
and wilt like cut flowers in the sun.**

Psalm 37:1-2 (The Message)

Do not get distracted by what appears to be the success of evil
or deceitful people. What is done in the dark will eventually
be revealed and destroyed by the light. God has a funny way
of humbling braggarts and people who seek to deceive others.
This usually seems to happen at just the right time.

Do not become intrigued by "get rich" schemes that prey on
others. Businesses that are built on shady foundations will
eventually crumble. Long standing success is built on
integrity, diligence, service, value, and honor.

Stay focused.
Be committed.
Operate with integrity.
Know that your faithfulness will be blessed.

Dear Lord,

I give you all honor, glory and praise for blessing me with life and the desire to build a business that serves you. Please help me focus on the Work that you have assigned to my life and keep me from being influenced by the boasting of others. As I look forward to a new week, I also ask...

Thank you for entrusting me with your Work.

_____   _____
Name   *Date*

Lesson 18 Affirmation

My business is built on a solid foundation of integrity. Integrity guides my every action.

My S.M.A.R.T. Goals for the Week Beginning: _____

SPECIFIC	**M**EASURABLE	**A**CTIONABLE	**R**ELEVANT	**T**IME-BOUND
This week I will: *<< insert goal >>*	I know that this goal has been accomplished when: *<insert description>*	I must take the following actions to make this goal a reality: 1.	Accomplishing this goal brings me closer to my vision of: *<insert short description of your vision>*	I will accomplish this goal by: *<insert day, date and time.>*
		2.		*This date should be within the next 7 days.
		3.		

83

LESSON 19

PUT GOD IN CHARGE

Put God in charge of your Work,
then what you've planned will take place.

Proverbs 16:3 (The Message)

When you put God in charge of your Work, what you have planned with God's guidance will happen.

Start by asking God to direct your path. Do this regardless of the stage that your business is in. Listen for God's instructions and write down what He reveals to you. God's revelation will provide the vision that will come to be the foundation for your plans and your Work.

Once you have co-created your plan for success with God through prayer and meditation - develop goals that are **s**pecific, **m**easurable, **a**ctionable, **r**elevant and **t**ime-bound (**S.M.A.R.T.**).

Work your plan through constant productive action. When your Work is done, rest in the knowledge that God is in charge of the result. In fact, the Bible says to put God in charge of your Work. When you do this your plans will be successful.

Be patient.
Be diligent.
Trust God.

Dear Lord,

I give you all honor, glory and praise for blessing me with life and the desire to build a business that serves you. Please guide me as I keep you first by reading your Word and following its instructions. As I look forward to a new week, I also ask…

Thank you for entrusting me with your Work.

_____   _____
Name   *Date*

Lesson 19 Affirmation

I am successful because God is in charge of my work.
I am at peace because God is in charge of my work.
I do not worry because God is in charge of my work.

My S.M.A.R.T. Goals for the Week Beginning:

SPECIFIC	**M**EASURABLE	**A**CTIONABLE	**R**ELEVANT	**T**IME-BOUND
This week I will: *<< insert goal >>*	I know that this goal has been accomplished when: *<insert description>*	I must take the following actions to make this goal a reality: 1. 2. 3.	Accomplishing this goal brings me closer to my vision of: *<insert short description of your vision>*	I will accomplish this goal by: *<insert day, date and time.>* *This date should be within the next 7 days.

LESSON 20

TREASURES IN SECRET PLACES

I will go before you and will level the mountains;
I will break down gates of bronze
and cut through bars of iron.

I will give you hidden treasures, riches stored in secret
places, so that you may know that I am the Lord, the God of
Israel, who summons you by name.

Isaiah 45:2-3   (NIV)

God will lead you through every obstacle and challenge that comes your way – if you let him.

God promises to clear a path to hidden treasures, riches stored in secret places, abundance and success that is beyond anything you could ever imagine. So, stop worrying about what is occurring or failing to occur in your business. Not only does God have your back, God promises to walk in front of you – leading you to the blessings He has ordained for your life.

Here is the exciting part: God says his blessings will not occur in secret. God promises to bless you in ways that make it crystal clear to you and those around you that your success is from God.

Do your Work with courage, confidence and boldness. Know that all things are working for your Good.

Dear Lord,

I give you all honor, glory and praise for blessing me with life and the desire to build a business that serves you. Thank you for helping me overcome every challenge that I face in my business. As I do your Work, please help me to see opportunities in all things. Help me to know and trust that every experience holds the possibility of being a hidden treasure that you have stored for me in a secret place. As I look forward to a new week, I also ask...

Thank you for entrusting me with your Work.

_____   _____
Name   *Date*

Lesson 20 Affirmation

My every action brings me closer to
the vision God has revealed to me.

My S.M.A.R.T. Goals for the Week Beginning:

SPECIFIC	MEASURABLE	ACTIONABLE	RELEVANT	TIME-BOUND
This week I will: << insert goal >>	I know that this goal has been accomplished when: <insert description>	I must take the following actions to make this goal a reality: 1. 2. 3.	Accomplishing this goal brings me closer to my vision of: <insert short description of your vision>	I will accomplish this goal by: <insert day, date and time.> *This date should be within the next 7 days.

LESSON 21

WRITE DOWN WHAT YOU SEE

And then God answered:
Write this. Write what you see.

Write it out in big block letters so
that it can be read on the run.
This vision-message is a witness pointing to what's coming –
it can hardly wait!
And it doesn't lie.

If it seems long in coming, wait.
It's on its way. It will come right on time.

Habakkuk 2:2-3 (The Message)

When God gives you a vision, write it down. Put copies of the vision that you have written down all around your home, office and car. Do this so you are reminded of your vision every day and every night.

After you have written your vision down on paper, go a step further and create a vision board. Do this by finding words and photos to make your vision vividly clear to you. Be sure to include images that depict both material and non-material desires – like family, friends and peace of mind. Paste these things on a poster board. Put your vision board in a place where you can see it every day and every night. Let your board be a visual reminder of what God has revealed to you.

Once you have written your vision down and created a vision board, make a list of exactly what needs to be done to make your vision a reality. In order to be effective, your list must be specific, measurable, actionable, relevant to your vision and limited by a time specific deadline (**S.M.A.R.T.**). Making a **S.M.A.R.T.** list is part of the "careful planning" the Bible says is necessary for success *(Proverbs 21:5)*.

After creating your **S.M.A.R.T.** list, write down the possible challenges you may face for everything you have listed. This will prepare you for the obstacles that will surely arise. Preparation will help you remain focused on your intended outcome in the face of adversity.

Now that you have a **S.M.A.R.T.** list of what is necessary to make your vision a reality, pull out your calendar and create a schedule for action. Action is how you transform God's *vision* for your life into the *reality* of your life.

Once you have written down what you need to succeed, surround yourself with people who are headed in the same direction as you – upward! You can do this by connecting with people in face-to-face settings, or locating and connecting with people in online communities. If you need help finding people to connect with online, start by following a few of our company Facebook pages:

www.Facebook.com/UpwardAction,
www.Facebook.com/PrayersOnDemand,
www.Facebook.com/MogulMoxie.

Once you have taken the **S.M.A.R.T.** actions necessary to make your vision a reality, God says to wait for your vision to be manifested. Be confident while you wait. Trust that your vision will be brought to life at just the right time – no matter how long the waiting takes.

Dear Lord,

I give you all honor, glory and praise for blessing me with life and the desire to build a business that serves you. Please guide my thoughts as I mediate on the vision you have given me. Help me to remain constant in taking the actions necessary to make my vision a reality while I wait on your timing for the results I continuously pray for and expect to receive. As I look forward to a new week, I also ask...

Thank you for entrusting me with your Work.

_____   _____
Name   *Date*

Lesson 21 Affirmation

My vision is becoming my reality.

My S.M.A.R.T. Goals for the Week Beginning:

SPECIFIC	**M**EASURABLE	**A**CTIONABLE	**R**ELEVANT	**T**IME-BOUND
This week I will: *<< insert goal >>*	I know that this goal has been accomplished when: *<insert description>*	I must take the following actions to make this goal a reality: 1. 2. 3.	Accomplishing this goal brings me closer to my vision of: *<insert short description of your vision>*	I will accomplish this goal by: *<insert day, date and time.>* *This date should be within the next 7 days.*

LESSON 22

GET READY FOR HIGH NOON

Open up before God, keep nothing back;
He'll do whatever needs to be done;
He'll validate your life in the clear light of day -
and stamp you with approval at high noon.

Psalm 37:5-6 (The Message)

To open up and give your all in business is not as easy as it sounds. It means delivering exceptional service at all times. It also requires you to provide value at every opportunity. Opening up and keeping nothing back means releasing all fear of failure and rejecting all feelings of inadequacy. The next step is to replace your fears with feelings of courageousness, love and self-discipline *(2 Timothy 1:7)*. Do these things and God has promised to do whatever needs to be done to ensure your success.

Here's the exciting part: your success will not be in secret. God promises to do whatever needs to be done on your behalf at high-noon – *which is the most creative, visible and advantageous time of your life.*

Stay encouraged.
Keep moving forward.
Trust that God has your back.
Know that Work done in the dark shows up in the light.

Dear Lord,

I give you all honor, glory and praise for blessing me with life and the desire to build a business that serves you. I lay all of my worry, concern and stress at your feet and leave them there. Please keep me grounded in your Word so that I am neither scared nor made arrogant by the ebbs and flows of business. As I look forward to a new week, I also ask...

Thank you for entrusting me with your Work.

_____   _____
Name   *Date*

Lesson 22 Affirmation

I give my best and my best is enough.

	My S.M.A.R.T. Goals for the Week Beginning:			
SPECIFIC	**M**EASURABLE	**A**CTIONABLE	**R**ELEVANT	**T**IME-BOUND
This week I will:	I know that this goal has been accomplished when:	I must take the following actions to make this goal a reality:	Accomplishing this goal brings me closer to my vision of:	I will accomplish this goal by:
<<insert goal>>	<insert description>	1.	<insert short description of your vision>	<insert day, date and time.>
		2.		*This date should be within the next 7 days.
		3.		

99

LESSON 23

DON'T HOLD BACK

Don't be afraid –
you're not going to be embarrassed.

Don't hold back –
You're not going to come up short.

Isaiah 54:4 (The Message)

Give your very best effort to whatever you want to accomplish in your business. When you refuse to hold back your best, God promises that you will not be embarrassed.

All too often, Christianpreneurs hold back their best efforts because of fear. They are afraid their best will not be good enough to win. By not giving 100%, these folks create an excuse to fail. Do not fall into this trap.

I encourage you to pour your heart into your business. Continuously improve the quality of the work your business provides to clients, customers and your target market.

Write your book.
Record your videos.
Develop your programs.
Provide your services.

Do these things knowing that in the long run you will not come up short.

In fact, when you consistently give your best in the spirit of excellence – your supporters will encourage you, your target market will invest with you, and above all else – God will bless you.

While you may not reach your sweet spot of success immediately, sustainable success and an influential legacy will be your reward if you keep moving forward.

Dear Lord,

I give you all honor, glory and praise for blessing me with life and the desire to build a business that serves you. Please give me the strength to aggressively confront my fears so they do not paralyze me with inaction. Help me to do the Work you have called me to do – even when it is hard and I am tired or afraid. As I look forward to a new week, I also ask...

Thank you for entrusting me with your Work.

_____   _____
Name   *Date*

Lesson 23 Affirmation

My prayers combined with my actions are creating lasting success.

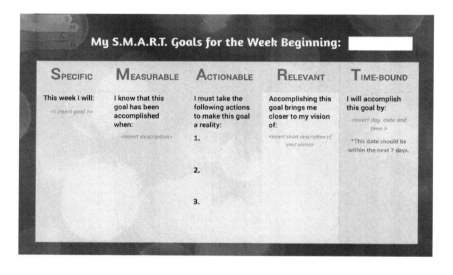

My S.M.A.R.T. Goals for the Week Beginning:

SPECIFIC	**M**EASURABLE	**A**CTIONABLE	**R**ELEVANT	**T**IME-BOUND
This week I will: *<< insert goal >>*	I know that this goal has been accomplished when: *<insert description>*	I must take the following actions to make this goal a reality: 1. 2. 3.	Accomplishing this goal brings me closer to my vision of: *<insert short description of your vision>*	I will accomplish this goal by: *<insert day, date and time.>* *This date should be within the next 7 days.

LESSON 24

DON'T QUIT!

Let us not become weary in doing good,
for at the proper time we will reap
a harvest if we do not give up.

Galatians 6:9 (NIV)

Building a profitable business that honors God, serves people, builds sustainable success and creates wealth is a marathon not a sprint. You may become weary during your journey, but do not quit.

I encourage you to continue doing what is necessary to grow your business, be innovative, and take your clients/customers to greater levels of success. Stay the course and refuse to give up. When you do these things, God promises that you will be successful at His appointed time.

Do good work.
Be encouraged.
Trust that God's blessings will be your reward.

Dear Lord,

I give you all honor, glory and praise for blessing me with life and the desire to build a business that serves you. During the times that I am tired, discouraged or even tempted to quit – help me stay focused on the many blessings I have already been given and your promise of what is to come. As I look forward to a new week, I also ask...

Thank you for entrusting me with your Work.

_____   _____
Name   *Date*

Lesson 24 Affirmation

I will finish what I start because my strength comes from the Lord.

My S.M.A.R.T. Goals for the Week Beginning: [_____]

SPECIFIC	MEASURABLE	ACTIONABLE	RELEVANT	TIME-BOUND
This week I will: <<insert goal >>	I know that this goal has been accomplished when: <insert description>	I must take the following actions to make this goal a reality: 1. 2. 3.	Accomplishing this goal brings me closer to my vision of: <insert short description of your vision>	I will accomplish this goal by: <insert day, date and time.> *This date should be within the next 7 days.

LESSON 25

MIND YOUR BUSINESS

Stay calm; mind your own business; do your own job.
You've heard all this from us before,
but a reminder never hurts.
We want you living in a way that will command the respect
of outsiders, not lying around
sponging off your friends.

1 Thessalonians 4:11-12 (The Message)

The first step in minding your business is to have business to mind. This simply means being clear about the Work you have been called to do *(aka – "your purpose" and "your God-Job")*. Once you know what you have been placed here on earth to accomplish and you are clear about the value that your business has been trusted by God to deliver, mind your business.

If you are stuck trying to figure out exactly what you have been created by God to do:

1. **Invest time in prayer and meditation.**
2. **Ask God to lead you to your purpose.**

Once you have done these things, invest in a spiritually grounded coach or mentor who can help guide your thoughts and ideas into actionable steps. This is important. When you know what your business is destined to do, you can focus on your Work.

Do not become distracted by what others are saying or doing around you. You have a job to do. Stay clear of petty things that are unproductive and do not move you forward. These things will murder your chances of leading a life and building a business that is respected by outsiders.

Do not waste your energy or God's time speaking ill of others. God has not made you judge and jury of the world; that is His job.

Resist any and all urges or temptations to denigrate people with negative talk or negative action. This will eventually rob you of your peace and the success you desire.

Focus on your Work.
Serve your clients.
Add value to your industry.

Be diligent about doing these things and you will earn the respect of the world around you. This respect will ultimately lead you to financial and soulful success. Give it a try.

Dear Lord,

I give you all honor, glory and praise for blessing me with life and the desire to build a business that serves you. Please send confirmation that the path I am on is in alignment with your will for my life. If not – please lead me to the Work that you would have me to do. As I look forward to a new week, I also ask...

Thank you for entrusting me with your Work.

_____   _____
Name   *Date*

Lesson 25 Affirmation

My business is bursting with success because I mind my business.

My S.M.A.R.T. Goals for the Week Beginning:

SPECIFIC	**M**EASURABLE	**A**CTIONABLE	**R**ELEVANT	**T**IME-BOUND
This week I will: *<< insert goal >>*	I know that this goal has been accomplished when: *<insert description>*	I must take the following actions to make this goal a reality: 1.	Accomplishing this goal brings me closer to my vision of: *<insert short description of your vision>*	I will accomplish this goal by: *<insert day, date and time.>* *This date should be within the next 7 days.*
		2.		
		3.		

LESSON 26

DON'T BE GULLIBLE

Don't suppress the Spirit, and don't stifle those who have a word from the Master.

On the other hand, don't be gullible.
Check out everything, keep only what's good.
Throw out anything tainted with evil.

1 Thessalonians 5:19-22 (The Message)

The most accomplished person in the room is often the quietest person in the room. The loudest person is often the fraudster. Pay attention to the verbal and non-verbal messages around you. Be humble enough to learn from those who have accomplished what you want to achieve. Listen to the advice you are given, determine what is best for you and then implement quickly.

Do not be influenced by liars and fools. If anything, use these types of people as examples of what not to do, regardless of how successful they may appear to be.

Do not get caught up in unnecessary drama. Operate your business with a sense of integrity. Develop a Christ-centered mission statement and code of ethics. Post these statements in places where they can be seen by both you and others – your website, lobby and internal offices are a few places that come to mind. A business that is built on character and honor can withstand the ebbs and flows of the market. A business that is compromised by misleading and deceitful practices will eventually fail.

Dear Lord,

I give you all honor, glory and praise for blessing me with life and the desire to build a business that serves you. Help me to be a person of integrity who does what is right, even when it is hard to do. As I look forward to a new week, I also ask...

Thank you for entrusting me with your Work.

_____   _____
Name   *Date*

Lesson 26 Affirmation

I attract wise counsel into my life.
The people around me inspire my best.
The people around me empower me to be my best.

My S.M.A.R.T. Goals for the Week Beginning: _____

SPECIFIC	MEASURABLE	ACTIONABLE	RELEVANT	TIME-BOUND
This week I will: *<< insert goal >>*	I know that this goal has been accomplished when: *<insert description>*	I must take the following actions to make this goal a reality: 1.	Accomplishing this goal brings me closer to my vision of: *<insert short description of your vision>*	I will accomplish this goal by: *<insert day, date and time.>* *This date should be within the next 7 days.*
		2.		
		3.		

LESSON 27

YOU ARE A BEACON

You are here to be light, ring out the God-colors in the world. God is not a secret to be kept.

We are going public with this, as public as a city on a hill.

If I make you light-bearers, you do not think I am going to hide you under a bucket, do you?
I am putting you on a light stand.

Now that I have put you there on a hilltop, on a light stand –shine!
Keep open house; be generous with your lives.

By opening up to others, you will prompt people to open up with God.

Matthew 5:14-16 (The Message)

Your business practices and you are both beacons of light to people who want to have more success in their business. Regardless of what stage your business is in - there is someone who is working hard to gain what you have already achieved. Never forget this.

Your faithfulness in making sacrifices and in doing what is necessary to build a profitable business that can withstand the tests of time is not going unnoticed.

People are watching you.
People are being inspired by you.

People are being encouraged to listen for the voice of God in their own lives because of your faithfulness. People are being motivated to pursue their own purpose because of your courageousness.

Your Work matters! You must never, ever forget this or take it for granted.

Keep shining.
Help others shine brighter.
Be the beacon of light that God intended for you to be.

Dear Lord,

I give you all honor, glory and praise for blessing me with life and the desire to build a business that serves you. Thank you for your Word, which shines light upon the dark places in my life and business. Please lead me to Christ-centered coaches and consultants who will be beacons of light for my business as I continue to be a beacon of light for those around me. As I look forward to a new week, I also ask...

Thank you for entrusting me with your Work.

_____   _____
Name   *Date*

Lesson 27 Affirmation

My faithfulness inspires others.
I am a beacon of light.

My S.M.A.R.T. Goals for the Week Beginning:				
SPECIFIC	**M**EASURABLE	**A**CTIONABLE	**R**ELEVANT	**T**IME-BOUND
This week I will: *<< insert goal >>*	I know that this goal has been accomplished when: *<insert description>*	I must take the following actions to make this goal a reality: 1.	Accomplishing this goal brings me closer to my vision of: *<insert short description of your vision>*	I will accomplish this goal by: *<insert day, date and time.>*
		2.		**This date should be within the next 7 days.*
		3.		

LESSON 28

WALK IN PROSPERITY

"For I know the plans I have for you," declares the Lord.
"Plans to prosper you and not to harm you,
plans to give you hope and a future.
Then you will call on me and come and pray to me,
and I will listen to you.
You will seek me and find me when you
seek me with all your heart."

Jeremiah 29:11-13 (NIV)

God has plans to bless you, prosper you and keep you from harm.

Stop wasting your time with worry when you do not think things are going your way. Know that God is with you. Trust that what is ahead of you is far greater than both what is currently happening in your life and what is behind you.

As you are building your business, seek the will of God in all that you do. Call on the Lord and share the desires of your heart. When you do this, God promises that he will come to you and listen to you.

When you seek God, you will find God.
When you find God, He will lead you.
When God leads you, you will find your purpose.

Dear Lord,

I give you all honor, glory and praise for blessing me with life and the desire to build a business that serves you. Thank you for wanting the best for me and for ensuring that all things are working for my good. As I look forward to a new week, I also ask...

Thank you for entrusting me with your Work.

_____   _____
Name   *Date*

Lesson 28 Affirmation

God hears my cries for help and listens to me.
I trust that all things are working for my good.

My S.M.A.R.T. Goals for the Week Beginning:

SPECIFIC	MEASURABLE	ACTIONABLE	RELEVANT	TIME-BOUND
This week I will: << insert goal >>	I know that this goal has been accomplished when: <insert description>	I must take the following actions to make this goal a reality: 1. 2. 3.	Accomplishing this goal brings me closer to my vision of: <insert short description of your vision>	I will accomplish this goal by: <insert day, date and time.> *This date should be within the next 7 days.

123

LESSON 29

YOU ARE NOT ALONE

In the same way I was with Moses, I'll be with you.
I won't give up on you; I won't leave you.
Strength! Courage!

Give it everything you have, heart and soul.
Don't get off track, either left or right, so as to make sure
you get to where you are going.

And don't for a minute let this Book of the Law
be out of mind.
Ponder and meditate on it day and night, making sure you
practice everything written in it.
Then you will get where you are going;
then you will succeed.

Haven't I commanded you?
Strength! Courage!
Don't be timid; don't get discouraged.
God, your God, is with your every step you take.

Joshua 1:5-9 (The Message)

Do not be discouraged by what you see around you. Do not
stress when things do not go as you have planned. Hold your
vision close to your soul. Meditate on the things that God has
told you. Think on them constantly. Focus on the tasks ahead.
Be consistent in taking action. Trust God with your heart and
mind. When God is your companion, all things are possible.

Here's the really good news: God will be your everlasting companion, if you ask.

God has promised to not give up on you.
So, don't YOU give up on you.
Keep moving forward.
Know that God is with you every step of your way.

Dear Lord,

I give you all honor, glory and praise for blessing me with life and the desire to build a business that serves you. Thank you for being with me throughout the highs and lows of business. I know that I can do all things through you, the provider of my strength. As I look forward to a new week, I also ask...

Thank you for entrusting me with your Work.

_____   _____
Name   *Date*

Lesson 29 Affirmation

My hope is built on the grace, mercy and power of God.

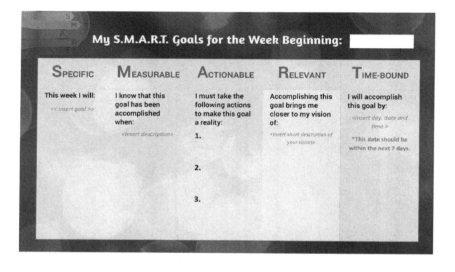

My S.M.A.R.T. Goals for the Week Beginning:

Specific	Measurable	Actionable	Relevant	Time-bound
This week I will: *<< insert goal >>*	I know that this goal has been accomplished when: *<insert description>*	I must take the following actions to make this goal a reality: 1. 2. 3.	Accomplishing this goal brings me closer to my vision of: *<insert short description of your vision>*	I will accomplish this goal by: *<insert day, date and time.>* *This date should be within the next 7 days.

LESSON 30

YOUR BUSINESS IS A TITHING

**So here is what I want you to do, God helping you;
Take your everyday, ordinary life -
your sleeping, eating, going-to-work, and walking around
life -
and place it before God as an offering.**

Romans 12:1 (The Message)

The journey to building a profitable business that is based on Christian principles may feel lonely; but, you are not alone.

God is helping you.
God is giving you strength.
God is opening doors for you.

Praise God for the vision that has become a business that serves people. Praise God for your ability to create wealth. Your praises are offerings to God.

Be diligent about taking the unglamorous actions necessary to move your business forward. I call this *"going to work"* in your business. Your diligence is an offering to God.

Be committed to the success of your clients, customers and those who come into contact with your business. Your commitment is an offering to God.

When you are faithful in treating the mundane, ordinary tasks necessary to build and operate the business of your dreams as a sacred offering to God - success will be inevitable.

Dear Lord,

I give you all honor, glory and praise for blessing me with life and the desire to build a business that serves you. Please help me maximize every opportunity that comes my way for I know my success is an offering to you and a testament to your grace, mercy and power. As I look forward to a new week, I also ask...

Thank you for entrusting me with your Work.

_____   _____
Name   *Date*

Lesson 30 Affirmation

I rejoice because God is blessing my Work and bringing my vision to life.

My S.M.A.R.T. Goals for the Week Beginning: [   ]

Specific	Measurable	Actionable	Relevant	Time-bound
This week I will:	I know that this goal has been accomplished when:	I must take the following actions to make this goal a reality:	Accomplishing this goal brings me closer to my vision of:	I will accomplish this goal by:
<< insert goal >>	*<insert description>*	1.	*<insert short description of your vision>*	*<insert day, date and time.>*
		2.		*This date should be within the next 7 days.*
		3.		

.

LESSON 31

DILIGENCE BRINGS WEALTH

**Lazy hands make for poverty,
but diligent hands bring wealth.**

Proverbs 10:4 (NIV)

It is easy to become so overwhelmed when thinking of all the things it takes to be successful that you become paralyzed with fear. Do not let this happen to you.

Get clear about what you want to accomplish in your business. Create a plan for the next 7 days, 30 days, 90 days and 365 days.

Once you know exactly what you want to accomplish, write down everything that must happen to bring your vision to life. When writing your list, make sure each item is specific, measurable, ready for action, relevant to your vision and time bound by a specific deadline (**S.M.A.R.T.**). This is the formula for creating goals that will lead you to success ... faster.

Now that you know what to do – pray harder and be diligent in executing your **S.M.A.R.T.** goals. God promises that your diligence will lead to your success.

Dear Lord,

I give you all honor, glory and praise for blessing me with life and the desire to build a business that serves you. Please guide me as I create **S.M.A.R.T.** goals that will move my business forward. Help me remain diligent in doing the Work required to make my goals a reality. As I look forward to a new week, I also ask...

Thank you for entrusting me with your Work.

_____   _____
Name   *Date*

Lesson 31 Affirmation

My diligence is leading to my wealth.

My S.M.A.R.T. Goals for the Week Beginning: _____

SPECIFIC	MEASURABLE	ACTIONABLE	RELEVANT	TIME-BOUND
This week I will: *<< insert goal >>*	I know that this goal has been accomplished when: *<insert description>*	I must take the following actions to make this goal a reality: 1. 2. 3.	Accomplishing this goal brings me closer to my vision of: *<insert short description of your vision>*	I will accomplish this goal by: *<insert day, date and time.>* *This date should be within the next 7 days.

LESSON 32

CALIBRATE YOUR ENERGY

**Indolence wants it all and gets nothing;
the energetic have something to show for their lives.**

Proverbs 13:4 (The Message)

If you are allergic to work, success will be allergic to you. If you want to win in business, you have to calibrate your energy levels and condition yourself for the win.

Here's how: invest more time with God, commit to consistent action, exercise an unrelenting desire to serve others, and - execute an incredible work ethic.

Your action will build the momentum you need to calibrate your energy. Your energy will drive your success.

Do not be a lazy dreamer.
Be an energetic visionary who makes things happen.

Dear Lord,

I give you all honor, glory and praise for blessing me with life and the desire to build a business that serves you. Thank you for the gift that is your Word for it refuels my energy and reignites my excitement for doing Your Work. As I look forward to a new week, I also ask...

Thank you for entrusting me with your Work.

_____   _____
Name   *Date*

Lesson 32 Affirmation

My positive energy blesses the life of everyone I encounter.

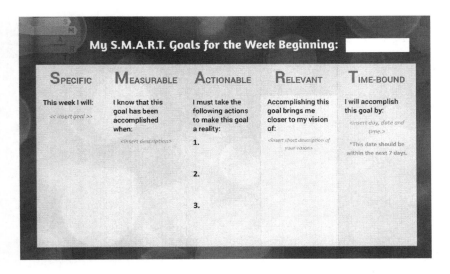

My S.M.A.R.T. Goals for the Week Beginning:

Sᴘᴇᴄɪꜰɪᴄ	Mᴇᴀꜱᴜʀᴀʙʟᴇ	Aᴄᴛɪᴏɴᴀʙʟᴇ	Rᴇʟᴇᴠᴀɴᴛ	Tɪᴍᴇ-ʙᴏᴜɴᴅ
This week I will: << insert goal >>	I know that this goal has been accomplished when: <insert description>	I must take the following actions to make this goal a reality: 1. 2. 3.	Accomplishing this goal brings me closer to my vision of: <insert short description of your vision>	I will accomplish this goal by: <insert day, date and time.> *This date should be within the next 7 days.

LESSON 33

DO YOUR WORK

*Make a careful exploration of who you are
and the work you have been given,
and then sink yourself into that.*

Don't compare yourself with others.

*Each of you must take responsibility
for doing the creative best you can with your own life.*

Galatians 6:4-5 (The Message)

Your clarity leads to your wealth. Get clear about the Work you have been called to do and sink yourself into it with reckless abandon. Trust that when you do this, your Work and your life will be blessed.

Here is how to start: you must first develop clarity about your vision, mission and goals. Clarity comes through prayer, meditation and collaboration with wise counsel. If you need help obtaining a clear understanding of what to do with your business, get help. The right coaches, consultants, mentors and/or experts can help you sift through the busyness of your business. These people can help you develop streamlined systems and processes to make your business more profitable and bring it into alignment with God's will. Ask God to lead wise counsel into your life.

Once you are clear about your God-given path, immerse yourself into doing the Work you have been called to do. Spend all of your working hours building a business that empowers your clients and customers to be better and experience more. Waste none of your time comparing yourself to others. Their purpose is not your purpose. Their journey is not for you.

Take responsibility for your own life and for your business. Do *your* Work and *trust* God to do the rest.

Dear Lord,

I give you all honor, glory and praise for blessing me with life and the desire to build a business that serves you. Help me to remain focused on the Work you have called me to do and not be distracted by the success or failures of others. Please help me celebrate the success of my friends and colleagues without envy – knowing that as long as I do my part, your will for my life will happen. As I look forward to a new week, I also ask…

Thank you for entrusting me with your Work.

_____   _____
Name   *Date*

Lesson 33 Affirmation

I am blessed and highly favored in all things and at all times.

My S.M.A.R.T. Goals for the Week Beginning:

SMART	**M**EASURABLE	**A**CTIONABLE	**R**ELEVANT	**T**IME-BOUND
This week I will:	I know that this goal has been accomplished when:	I must take the following actions to make this goal a reality:	Accomplishing this goal brings me closer to my vision of:	I will accomplish this goal by:
<< insert goal >>	<insert description>	1.	<insert short description of your vision>	<insert day, date and time.>
		2.		*This date should be within the next 7 days.
		3.		

144

LESSON 34

STOP CHASING

The one who stays on the job has food on the table;
the witless chase whims and fancies.

Proverbs 12:11 (The Message)

Consistent, focused action is key to being in the flow of success. Distractions like the "latest and greatest" program, product or service in your industry *(aka "whims and fancies")* will lead to failure. Giving in to such distractions is the behavior of the foolish and the poor.

Do not waste your time chasing dreams and lofty ideas that are not rooted in specific, measurable, actionable, relevant and time-bound (**S.M.A.R.T.**) objectives.

Instead, take time to prayerfully develop a plan of action that will help you accomplish the goals necessary for success. Once your plan has been established, stay on the job of making your goals a reality by exercising self-discipline and diligent action.

When you do these things, you will always have enough "food on the table" for your household and enough to give away to charity too.

Dear Lord,

I give you all honor, glory and praise for blessing me with life and the desire to build a business that serves you. Please be with me and guide me as I take the steps necessary to make my business successful and my vision a reality. As I look forward to a new week, I also ask...

Thank you for entrusting me with your Work.

_____   _____
Name   *Date*

Lesson 34 Affirmation

My self-discipline and diligence attracts my ideal clients, customers, mentors and advisors to me.

My S.M.A.R.T. Goals for the Week Beginning:				
SPECIFIC	**M**EASURABLE	**A**CTIONABLE	**R**ELEVANT	**T**IME-BOUND
This week I will: *<< insert goal >>*	I know that this goal has been accomplished when: *<insert description>*	I must take the following actions to make this goal a reality: 1.	Accomplishing this goal brings me closer to my vision of: *<insert short description of your vision>*	I will accomplish this goal by: *<insert day, date and time.>* *This date should be within the next 7 days.*
		2.		
		3.		

LESSON 35

STEADY WINS THE RACE

Easy come, easy go,
but steady diligence pays off.

Proverbs 13:11 (The Message)

Do not be the kind of fickle businessperson who wastes time, energy and resources chasing after the "latest and greatest" things promoted in the marketplace.

Do not become distracted by people, programs, products and services that promise incredible results with very little effort. "Get rich quick" is not sustainable.

If you want to be successful in business, create detailed plans of actions that are based on goals that are specific, measurable, actionable, relevant and bound by time (**S.M.A.R.T.**). Some of your plans of action should contain short-term goals while others must contain long-term projects. Both types require time and consistency that will pay off if you engage in "steady diligence."

Once your foundation is firm, you will be in a position to experiment with the "latest and greatest" programs, products or services without wasting too much time or otherwise damaging your business. When you first focus on a proven course of action and *only then* experiment with the unknown, success will be your reward.

Dear Lord,

I give you all honor, glory and praise for blessing me with life and the desire to build a business that serves you. Please give me the discernment I need to separate good from bad, true from false, and real from fake. Help me avoid all scams and schemes that would lead me astray. As I look forward to a new week, I also ask...

Thank you for entrusting me with your Work.

_____   _____
Name   *Date*

Lesson 35 Affirmation

All of my actions lead to profitable returns; no effort is wasted.

My S.M.A.R.T. Goals for the Week Beginning:

Specific	Measurable	Actionable	Relevant	Time-bound
This week I will: *<< insert goal >>*	I know that this goal has been accomplished when: *<insert description>*	I must take the following actions to make this goal a reality: 1. 2. 3.	Accomplishing this goal brings me closer to my vision of: *<insert short description of your vision>*	I will accomplish this goal by: *<insert day, date and time.>* *This date should be within the next 7 days.*

LESSON 36

AVOID THE RUINS

The integrity of the honest keeps them on track;
the deviousness of crooks brings them to ruins.

Proverbs 11:3 (The Message)

Give your very best to every person who invests in your business. This includes people who have purchased your programs, products and services – as well as those who consume your free content on social media platforms or in publications. Never forget that the time people give you is invaluable and once spent is gone forever, so honor it.

When you give generously to your online and offline communities, the people you encounter will reward you with sales, testimonials, endorsements and referrals.

When you give less than your best – or you are deceitful and underhanded - it is only a matter of time before everything crumbles around you.

The Word says that honesty and integrity will keep you on track. It also says deviousness and crookedness will lead to ruin. Therefore, make excellence your hallmark and your business will prosper.

Dear Lord,

I give you all honor, glory and praise for blessing me with life and the desire to build a business that serves you. Please help me stay committed to building a business that is based on integrity. Keep me protected from shady people and questionable situations. As I look forward to a new week, I also ask…

Thank you for entrusting me with your Work.

_____   _____
Name   *Date*

Lesson 36 Affirmation

Every action I take is for the greater good of everyone involved.

My S.M.A.R.T. Goals for the Week Beginning:				
SPECIFIC	**M**EASURABLE	**A**CTIONABLE	**R**ELEVANT	**T**IME-BOUND
This week I will: *<< insert goal >>*	I know that this goal has been accomplished when: *<insert description>*	I must take the following actions to make this goal a reality: 1.	Accomplishing this goal brings me closer to my vision of: *<insert short description of your vision>*	I will accomplish this goal by: *<insert day, date and time.>* *This date should be within the next 7 days.
		2.		
		3.		

LESSON 37

MAKE SURE YOU UNDERSTAND IT

Now this is our boast:
Our conscience testifies that we have conducted ourselves in
the world and especially in our relations with you,
with integrity and godly sincerity.

We have done so, relying not on worldly wisdom but on
God's grace. For we do not write you anything you cannot
read or understand.

2 Corinthians 1:12 (NIV)

Integrity and godly sincerity are two required ingredients for a life that honors God and serves you. The business of a Christianpreneur is one that operates with integrity and prioritizes transparency by not hiding key information in the fine print. To be transparent is to be upfront with your clients, customers, vendors, suppliers, staff, team members and other business partners. To be sincere is to conduct business with an intention to provide exceptional value in return for payment.

When godly sincerity is at the heart of your business, your ideal clients will be drawn to you and God's grace will be upon you.

A business of integrity is a business that honors God.
A business that honors God is a business that builds legacy.
A business that builds legacy is a business that will generate wealth in the years to come.

Dear Lord,

I give you all honor, glory and praise for blessing me with life and the desire to build a business that serves you. Help me prioritize transparency and forthrightness in my business so the Work I do is an accurate reflection of your love, grace and mercy. As I look forward to a new week, I also ask…

Thank you for entrusting me with your Work.

_____   _____
Name   *Date*

Lesson 37 Affirmation

I am always honest with those
who invest in my business.
My business honors God, serves
people and builds wealth.

My S.M.A.R.T. Goals for the Week Beginning:				
SPECIFIC	**M**EASURABLE	**A**CTIONABLE	**R**ELEVANT	**T**IME-BOUND
This week I will: *<< insert goal >>*	I know that this goal has been accomplished when: *<insert description>*	I must take the following actions to make this goal a reality: 1.	Accomplishing this goal brings me closer to my vision of: *<insert short description of your vision>*	I will accomplish this goal by: *<insert day, date and time.>* *This date should be within the next 7 days.*
		2.		
		3.		

LESSON 38

HONOR YOUR STAFF

Don't abuse a laborer who is destitute and needy, whether he is a fellow Israelite living in your land and in your city.

Pay him at the end of each workday; he's living from hand to mouth and needs it now.

If you hold back his pay, he'll protest to God and you will have sin on your books.

Deuteronomy 24:14-15 (The Message)

Do not cheat, swindle or otherwise mistreat your employees, contractors, vendors or interns. Never shortchange or otherwise deceive the people who work for you. Deliver to others what you have promised to deliver and do it when you have promised to do it. Do not let your actions disrupt anyone's life.

God's Word requires you to be honest, fair and trustworthy to the people who work for you. This is key to building a team that is both committed and highly productive. Effective team building also requires that you quickly fire people who are not doing a good job and take really good care of the people who make your business run smoothly. Do this and your business will not only prosper, you will rest easy knowing the people who work for you are loyal to you.

Dear Lord,

I give you all honor, glory and praise for blessing me with life and the desire to build a business that serves you. Help me to be intentional about caring for my staff in ways that will help them both be their best and also add tremendous value to my company. Please bless my business with financial resources that make it possible for me to be a blessing to my team. As I look forward to a new week, I also ask...

Thank you for entrusting me with your Work.

_____   _____
Name   *Date*

Lesson 38 Affirmation

I am a fantastic boss;
people love to work for me.

My S.M.A.R.T. Goals for the Week Beginning: ☐

SPECIFIC	**M**EASURABLE	**A**CTIONABLE	**R**ELEVANT	**T**IME-BOUND
This week I will:	I know that this goal has been accomplished when:	I must take the following actions to make this goal a reality:	Accomplishing this goal brings me closer to my vision of:	I will accomplish this goal by:
<< insert goal >>	<insert description>	1.	<insert short description of your vision>	<insert day, date and time.>
		2.		*This date should be within the next 7 days.
		3.		

163

LESSON 39

BREATHE LIFE

The very moment that you separate body and spirit, you end up with a corpse.

Separate faith and works and you get the same thing: a corpse.

James 2:26 (The Message)

Just as a body must contain spirit to have life, your faith must be supported by your "works" in order for you to experience financial success.

When you include Christ in making plans for your business and are consistent in doing your Work, your efforts will not be wasted nor will they be in vain.

It is time to breathe life into your business. Here's how:

Commit to doing the Work you know is necessary for success. Believe that God will bless your work.

Now that you know what to do – it is time for your upward action. Get going.

Dear Lord,

I give you all honor, glory and praise for blessing me with life and the desire to build a business that serves you. Please provide all I need to design and implement "Works" in my business that are effective, profitable and of service to your kingdom. As I look forward to a new week, I also ask...

Thank you for entrusting me with your Work.

_____   _____
Name   *Date*

Lesson 39 Affirmation

God gives life to my business.
My life gives meaning to my business.
My business brings joy to my life.

My S.M.A.R.T. Goals for the Week Beginning: _____

Specific	Measurable	Actionable	Relevant	Time-Bound
This week I will: ‹‹ insert goal ››	I know that this goal has been accomplished when: ‹insert description›	I must take the following actions to make this goal a reality: 1. 2. 3.	Accomplishing this goal brings me closer to my vision of: ‹insert short description of your vision›	I will accomplish this goal by: ‹insert day, date and time.› *This date should be within the next 7 days.

LESSON 40

TAKE IT SERIOUSLY

**It pays to take life seriously;
things work out when you trust in God.**

Proverbs 16:20 (The Message)

Success is elusive to many business owners because they are playing at business – not doing business. Playing at business happens when you do not have things like systems, benchmarks for financial success and accountability built into your corporate structure.

If you want God to bless your business, you have got to take it seriously. Develop the systems and hire the people necessary to accomplish business goals that are specific, measurable, actionable, relevant and bound by time (**S.M.A.R.T.**).

Taking your business seriously also means being prayerful about every decision and taking fast action once a decision has been made.

Pray.
Listen.
Act.
Repeat.

When you take the upward action necessary to make your business a success and trust God to bless your actions – expect to experience the blessings God has in store for you.

Dear Lord,

I give you all honor, glory and praise for blessing me with life and the desire to build a business that serves you. Please guide me and help me obtain the knowledge I need to build a business that adds value to the world, serves God and creates wealth. As I look forward to a new week, I also ask...

Thank you for entrusting me with your Work.

_____   _____
Name   *Date*

Lesson 40 Affirmation

My actions show that I am serious about building a Christ-centered business that serves people and honors God.

My S.M.A.R.T. Goals for the Week Beginning:				
SPECIFIC	**M**EASURABLE	**A**CTIONABLE	**R**ELEVANT	**T**IME-BOUND
This week I will: *<< insert goal >>*	I know that this goal has been accomplished when: *<insert description>*	I must take the following actions to make this goal a reality: 1. 2. 3.	Accomplishing this goal brings me closer to my vision of: *<insert short description of your vision>*	I will accomplish this goal by: *<insert day, date and time.>* *This date should be within the next 7 days.

LESSON 41

SECRETS TO INCREASE

For I command you today to:
Love the Lord your God,
Walk in obedience to Him, and
Keep his commands, decrees and laws;
Then you will live and increase,
and the Lord your God will bless you
in the land you are entering to possess.

Deuteronomy 30:16 (NIV)

You have been placed in the world to fulfill a special purpose that has been created just for you.

As a Christianpreneur, you have been called by God to build a business that positively impacts the lives of the people who encounter it. This is true regardless of your industry. Law practices, restaurants, beauty salons, managed health care services, executive coaching practices, consultancies and financial service firms are examples of various types of businesses that serve people and can reflect a spirit of excellence and service that ultimately gives God glory.

Build your business on Christian principles.
Operate your business with integrity.
Do the Work you have been called to do with excellence.

When you are obedient in following God's commandments, you can rest in knowing that you will experience the reward of God's blessings in God's appointed time.

Dear Lord,

I give you all honor, glory and praise for blessing me with life and the desire to build a business that serves you. Please grant me the ability to dissect life and business lessons from your Word. When I am tempted to do things that are not in alignment with your will, please send reminders of your purpose for my life. As I look forward to a new week, I also ask…

Thank you for entrusting me with your Work.

_____   _____
Name   *Date*

Lesson 41 Affirmation

I am obedient to God and God is faithful to me.

My S.M.A.R.T. Goals for the Week Beginning:

SPECIFIC	MEASURABLE	ACTIONABLE	RELEVANT	TIME-BOUND
This week I will: << insert goal >>	I know that this goal has been accomplished when: <insert description>	I must take the following actions to make this goal a reality: 1.	Accomplishing this goal brings me closer to my vision of: <insert short description of your vision>	I will accomplish this goal by: <insert day, date and time.> *This date should be within the next 7 days.
		2.		
		3.		

175

LESSON 42

GET READY AND RUN!

Trust God from the bottom of your heart;
don't try to figure out everything on your own.

Listen for God's voice in everything you do, everywhere you
go; He's the One who will keep you on track.

Don't assume that you know it all.
Run to God! Run from evil!
Your body will glow with health,
your very bones will vibrate with life.

Proverbs 3:5-8 (The Message)

You do not have to figure out what it takes to be successful in business all by yourself.

The Bible provides instruction for what to do:

Ask God for guidance.
Hire wise counsel and follow their advice.
Commit your plans to God.
Trust that what you have planned will happen.

When you do these things, the Word promises that your business will grow and vibrate with the health of success.

Dear Lord,

I give you all honor, glory and praise for blessing me with life and the desire to build a business that serves you. Please clear my ears so I can hear your voice. Help me attract wise counsel into my business and my life so I do not stray from the path that leads to my divine purpose. As I look forward to a new week, I also ask...

Thank you for entrusting me with your Work.

_____   _____
Name   *Date*

Lesson 42 Affirmation

I am running to God and my life is glowing with the vibrant health of success.

My S.M.A.R.T. Goals for the Week Beginning:

SPECIFIC	**M**EASURABLE	**A**CTIONABLE	**R**ELEVANT	**T**IME-BOUND
This week I will: *<< insert goal >>*	I know that this goal has been accomplished when: *<insert description>*	I must take the following actions to make this goal a reality: 1.	Accomplishing this goal brings me closer to my vision of: *<insert short description of your vision>*	I will accomplish this goal by: *<insert day, date and time.>* *This date should be within the next 7 days.
		2.		
		3.		

LESSON 43

THE FIRST FRUITS

Honor God with everything that you own;
give Him the first and the best.

Your barns will burst,
your wine vats will brim over.

Proverbs 3:8-10 (The Message)

The abundance that flows from your business is not for you alone. Your business is a representative of God's glory. Your success is a testimony for what God can and will do in accordance with His will. These things are true regardless of the amount of success you feel that you are or are not experiencing right now.

Honor God with the first and best fruits of your labor. There are lots of ways to do this. Support your church. Donate to civic organizations that are doing the work of the Lord. Add value to the lives of people around you – and do it without judgment. Treat all people with a respect that allows others to experience the spirit of God through your actions.

When you give God the first and best of your labor by doing these things, God promises that abundance will be your reward.

Dear Lord,

I give you all honor, glory and praise for blessing me with life and the desire to build a business that serves you. Please help me put you first at all times and in everything I do. Help me to be generous in sharing my money, my talents, my knowledge and my life experiences with those who need and seek my help. As I look forward to a new week, I also ask...

Thank you for entrusting me with your Work.

_____   _____
Name   *Date*

Lesson 43 Affirmation

My life is a reflection of God's grace.

My S.M.A.R.T. Goals for the Week Beginning:

Specific	Measurable	Actionable	Relevant	Time-bound
This week I will: << insert goal >>	I know that this goal has been accomplished when: <insert description>	I must take the following actions to make this goal a reality: 1. 2. 3.	Accomplishing this goal brings me closer to my vision of: <insert short description of your vision>	I will accomplish this goal by: <insert day, date and time.> *This date should be within the next 7 days.

183

LESSON 44

MAKE TIME TO REST

Work for six days, and rest the seventh,
so your ox and donkey may rest -
and your servant and migrant workers
may have time to get their needed rest.

Exodus 23:12 (The Message)

Be willing to work around the clock as instructed in Ecclesiastes 11:6 and also set aside time for rest. Proper rest is essential for sustainable success. This is true for both you and the people who work for you. Requiring your staff to work around the clock is not only ineffective, it contradicts God's instruction for how we as Christianpreneurs are to live our lives and run our businesses.

Get into compliance with the Word of God by insisting that everyone who works in your organization makes time to rest at least one day a week. When people are rested, they are more creative and effective. When you are rested, you are more creative and strategic.

Build rest into the culture of your company and not only will your staff thank you - your mind, body and spirit will reward you.

Dear Lord,

I give you all honor, glory and praise for blessing me with life and the desire to build a business that serves you. Please help me develop a deeper trust in you so I can work less and rest more without fear of missing out. As I look forward to a new week, I also ask…

Thank you for entrusting me with your Work.

_____   _____
Name   *Date*

Lesson 44 Affirmation

I honor my staff with time to rest and they honor me with productive work and loyalty.

My S.M.A.R.T. Goals for the Week Beginning: _____

SPECIFIC	MEASURABLE	ACTIONABLE	RELEVANT	TIME-BOUND
This week I will: << insert goal >>	I know that this goal has been accomplished when: <insert description>	I must take the following actions to make this goal a reality: 1. 2. 3.	Accomplishing this goal brings me closer to my vision of: <insert short description of your vision>	I will accomplish this goal by: <insert day, date and time.> *This date should be within the next 7 days.

LESSON 45

YOUR GIFTS WILL MAKE ROOM

A gift opens the way
and ushers the giver into the presence of great people.

Proverbs 18:16(NIV)

A gift gets attention;
it buys the attention of eminent people.

Proverbs 18:16 (The Message)

PART ONE: **SHARE YOUR GIFTS**

You have a talent. You. Yes, you! Your talent is something you naturally do well and love so much you would do it for free. Your talent is a gift from God. The Bible makes it clear that your gifts will create a space for you, usher you into the presence of great people, and bring forth unexpected and amazing opportunities.

In order for your gifts to open doors and lead you into greatness, there is work to do. You must be excited about being of service to your target market; committed to developing your gifts and making your good, great; diligent about sharing your gifts with the world around you; and courageous enough to not only place a value on your gifts – but also require payment.

Do not take the gift that is your talent for granted. What is easy for you is hard for someone else. People need for you to do what is easy for you. In fact, there are people who are literally waiting for you to release your gifts *(aka "your light")* so their lives can be transformed – many of these people do not even know it yet. Do not keep these people, your ideal clients, waiting in the dark. When you are diligent about sharing your God-given gifts through doing the Work you have been called to do, God promises that your gifts will create the space needed to attract opportunities that will astound you.

So - stop holding back. God did not give you a spirit of the timid - but of self-discipline, love and power *(2 Timothy 1:7).* Share your gifts, shine your light and transform the world.

PART TWO: **GIVE GIFTS**

Eminent *(aka "influential")* people are those held in high regard by others. These are the people who can help your business go further, faster. Influential people in your life include mentors, coaches, consultants, friends, family, clients, customers, celebrities, leaders in government and leaders in business who you may not know personally, but admire from afar.

The Word says gifts will buy the attention of *eminent* people. A gift is something of value that is given without expectation of payment. It can be a physical item or something intangible like time, an act of kindness or even advice.

If you are ready to attract the attention of *eminent* people who can help move your business forward, start by making a list of the people you admire, who can help you achieve your goals. Pay attention to what these people are doing online and offline. Based on what you learn, write down specific ways you can help these folks accomplish their goals. The things you write down are your gifts.

Once you are clear about how you can give "gifts" to the people you have written on your list, get busy distributing your gifts *(some for free, others for a fee)*. When you do this consistently, a healthy portion of these people will start to notice you. Once they begin to notice you, be ready to leverage the attention.

Dear Lord,

I give you all honor, glory and praise for blessing me with life and the desire to build a business that serves you. Please help me find new opportunities to share my gifts in ways that are a blessing to others. Keep me grounded in the knowledge that so long as I use my gifts to honor you, they will open doors to more and more opportunities. Expand my mind as I write the names of people who can help me and I can also help. Give me the courage to make the first contact with everyone on my list or guide these people to contact me. As I look forward to a new week, I also ask...

Thank you for entrusting me with your Work.

_____   _____
Name   *Date*

Lesson 45 Affirmation

My actions attract blessings and favor from
God and influential people.
My gifts are opening doors of opportunities for me.
My gifts are transforming the world.

My S.M.A.R.T. Goals for the Week Beginning:

Specific	Measurable	Actionable	Relevant	Time-Bound
This week I will: << insert goal >>	I know that this goal has been accomplished when: <insert description>	I must take the following actions to make this goal a reality: 1. 2. 3.	Accomplishing this goal brings me closer to my vision of: <insert short description of your vision>	I will accomplish this goal by: <insert day, date and time.> *This date should be within the next 7 days.

LESSON 46

DON'T BE INTIMIDATED

They were trying to intimidate us into quitting.

They thought:
"They'll give up and never finish it."
I prayed: "Give me strength."

Nehemiah 6:9 (The Message)

The success you desire may seem far away; but do not quit. Projects may not be going as planned; stay the course.

You may feel the world is out to destroy what you have worked so hard to create; do not be discouraged.

People who do not support or believe in you may be out in full force; ignore them.

Know that God gives you strength and God has the power to bless your business. While human beings can certainly create challenges you will have to overcome, no man or woman can destroy what God has planned for your business and your life. The power for this type of destruction belongs to you. Do not exercise it by becoming discouraged because of delays you encounter on your way to success or quitting before you have completed the Work that God has assigned for your life.

Ask God for guidance.
P A U S E and listen for instruction.
Do the Work God tells you to do.
Expect to succeed.

Dear Lord,

I give you all honor, glory and praise for blessing me with life and the desire to build a business that serves you. Please send inspiration my way when I am discouraged. When I feel like quitting, help me remember that building the business of my dreams takes time and requires much patience. As I look forward to a new week, I also ask...

Thank you for entrusting me with your Work.

_____   _____
Name   *Date*

Lesson 46 Affirmation

I am supported by the love of God.
I am successful by the grace of God.

My S.M.A.R.T. Goals for the Week Beginning:

SPECIFIC	MEASURABLE	ACTIONABLE	RELEVANT	TIME-BOUND
This week I will: *<< insert goal >>*	I know that this goal has been accomplished when: *<insert description>*	I must take the following actions to make this goal a reality: 1. 2. 3.	Accomplishing this goal brings me closer to my vision of: *<insert short description of your vision>*	I will accomplish this goal by: *<insert day, date and time.>* *This date should be within the next 7 days.*

197

LESSON 47

KILL THE "IF"

Jesus said, "If?"
There are no "Ifs" among believers.
Anything can happen."

Mark 9:23 (The Message)

You are going to be successful in business! You have got to believe this if it is going to happen for you. Even a seed of doubt will grow, fester, and ultimately destroy what you are working to create. Jesus says that among believers anything can happen. Take a moment and let this verse seep into your consciousness.

If you are a believer and you are feeling the pressures of being in business, stop doubting that what you are working to build is possible. Always remember that with the power of God, anything is possible. This is God's Word to Christianpreneurs. *(God is talking to you!)*

Believe God.
Limit time with those who don't support your vision.
Surround yourself with positive people.
Know that everything is possible.
Trust that anything can happen.

Dear Lord,

I give you all honor, glory and praise for blessing me with life and the desire to build a business that serves you. Please give me the confidence I need to boldly claim victory in every area of my life. Help me internalize the knowledge that through Christ Jesus all things are possible. As I look forward to a new week, I also ask...

Thank you for entrusting me with your Work.

_____   _____
Name   *Date*

Lesson 47 Affirmation

I know that through the power of God anything and everything is possible.

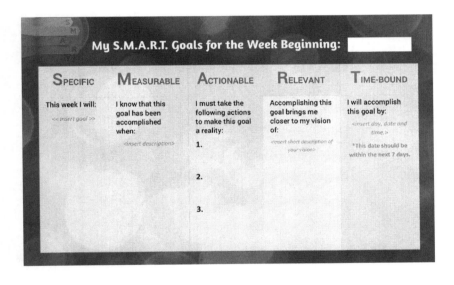

LESSON 48

LEAVE SOME EXTRA

When you reap the harvest of your land, do not reap to the very edges of your field or gather the gleanings of your harvest.

Do not go over your vineyard a second time or pick up the grapes that have fallen. Leave them for the poor and the foreigner.

Leviticus 19:9-10 (NIV)

God requires you to share a portion of what you have with people who are less fortunate. Regardless of whether you are in a season of abundance or you feel that you are barely making ends meet, you have something that can bless someone else.

If you do not know what you have to give – I have a solution. Conduct an assessment of your money, time, knowledge and positive energy. Decide what portion of these things you can give to someone else.

Once you know what you have to give, write down exactly what you are willing to give away. Then, open up your day planner to schedule your giving. The next step is to G I V E!

When you are intentional about being charitable to others, you will find that God will be amazingly charitable to you. Give it a try.

Dear Lord,

I give you all honor, glory and praise for blessing me with life and the desire to build a business that serves you. Please help me to always be mindful that what I sow in others I will eventually reap. Never let me forget that giving to those who are less fortunate is proof of my faithfulness to you and adherence to your Word. As I look forward to a new week, I also ask...

Thank you for entrusting me with your Work.

_____   _____
Name   *Date*

Lesson 48 Affirmation

I find creative ways to support those around me.

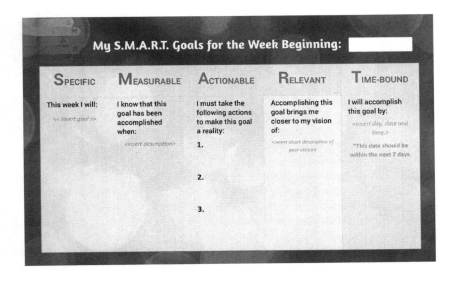

LESSON 49

MAKE IT KNOWN

Ask and it will be given to you;
seek and you will find;
knock and the door will be opened to you.
For everyone who asks receives;
the one who seeks find;
and to the one who knocks, the door will be opened.

Matthew 7:7 (NIV)

So I say to you: Ask and it will be given to you;
seek and you will find;
knock and the door will be opened to you.
For everyone who asks receives;
the one who seeks finds;
and to the one who knocks, the door will be opened.

Luke 11:9 (NIV)

Action is critically important to success. Being proactive about success is so important; God provides detailed instructions for how to get what you want twice – first in Matthew and then in Luke.

If you want to experience increase in your business, ask.

Ask God for guidance.
Ask your ideal clients to invest.
Ask the people who respect and admire you to refer business.

If you want your business to grow, seek.

Seek the voice of God in every decision you make.
Seek wisdom so you know what to do and when to do it.
Seek peace so you are not anxious as you move about your day, but are confident in the knowledge that God will provide your every need.

If you want to experience exponential success, knock.

Knock on the doors of mentors to plan your success.
Knock on the doors of influencers to expand your territory.
Knock on the doors of advisors to accelerate your success.

When you do these things and the desires of your heart are aligned with God's will for your life: you will receive that for which you have asked, you will find what you are seeking, and doors will be opened to you.

Dear Lord,

I give you all honor, glory and praise for blessing me with life and the desire to build a business that serves you. Please grant me the ability to get help when I need it by asking, seeking, and knocking. Release me from all fear of rejection so I can boldly approach the wise counsel you have placed in my path for help on my journey of doing the Work you have called me to do. As I look forward to a new week, I also ask...

Thank you for entrusting me with your Work.

_____   _____
Name   *Date*

Lesson 49 Affirmation

I am blessed and highly favored. God hears my requests and my desires become my reality.

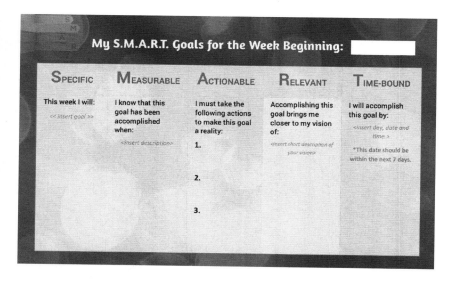

My S.M.A.R.T. Goals for the Week Beginning:

SPECIFIC	**M**EASURABLE	**A**CTIONABLE	**R**ELEVANT	**T**IME-BOUND
This week I will:	I know that this goal has been accomplished when:	I must take the following actions to make this goal a reality:	Accomplishing this goal brings me closer to my vision of:	I will accomplish this goal by:
<< insert goal >>	*<insert description>*	1.	*insert short description of your vision>*	*<insert day, date and time.>*
		2.		*This date should be within the next 7 days.*
		3.		

LESSON 50

BE STRATEGIC

**Strategic planning is the key to warfare;
to win, you need a lot of good counsel.**

Psalm 24:6 (The Message)

Fail to plan, and you plan to fail. If you want to win in business and in life, you have to be clear about what it takes to succeed. The fastest way to be successful is to work with subject matter experts who are skilled in what you want to accomplish.

Identify leaders in the areas you want to experience success. Spend time consuming their content through articles, podcasts, interviews, social media and blogs. Interact with them online and/or off-line *(when possible)*. Once you have learned essential details about the skills, expertise and temperament of the people you admire and you have used what you have learned to identify a person who can help you get to your next level of success, hire that person. Start with one.

If you do not currently have a mentor or coach, make this the week you start the process of finding the right counsel for your business and/or life.

If you have a coach or mentor who is helping you experience success in one area of your life or business, determine in what other areas you need to grow. Once you know where you need to experience growth, find wise counsel to help accelerate success in those areas.

Dear Lord,

I give you all honor, glory and praise for blessing me with life and the desire to build a business that serves you. Help me to become more strategic in my business planning. Please also help me attract wise counsel who will advise me on my journey to success. As I look forward to a new week, I also ask...

Thank you for entrusting me with your Work.

_____   _____
Name   *Date*

Lesson 50 Affirmation

I am surrounded by people who support
my vision and my dreams.

My S.M.A.R.T. Goals for the Week Beginning: _____

SPECIFIC	**M**EASURABLE	**A**CTIONABLE	**R**ELEVANT	**T**IME-BOUND
This week I will: *<< insert goal >>*	I know that this goal has been accomplished when: *<insert description>*	I must take the following actions to make this goal a reality: 1.	Accomplishing this goal brings me closer to my vision of: *<insert short description of your vision>*	I will accomplish this goal by: *<insert day, date and time.>* *This date should be within the next 7 days.*
		2.		
		3.		

LESSON 51

REJECT THE BACKSEAT

Observe those who are skilled in their work –
skilled workers are always in demand and admired;
they don't take a backseat to anyone.

Proverbs 22:29 (The Message)

To enjoy the success that flows from a profitable business, become the very best at what you do.

Start by exceeding the expectations of your clients and customers. This happens when you provide exceptional service. It also happens when you are consistent in creating outstanding content especially for your ideal clients. The content that you create can be published through special reports, articles and blog posts that you provide for free *(or in exchange for contact information)* - as well as in programs and products. Automate this process whenever possible.

When excellence becomes your hallmark:

Your clients will refer business to you.
Your reputation will attract your ideal clients.
Your competition will disappear.

Do the work necessary to become the best and trust God to do the rest.

Dear Lord,

I give you all honor, glory and praise for blessing me with life and the desire to build a business that serves you. Please help me provide exceptional value at every opportunity for I know that the love and care I show my clients and customers helps them to experience the love and care that you show me. As I look forward to a new week, I also ask...

Thank you for entrusting me with your Work.

_____   _____
Name   *Date*

216

Lesson 51 Affirmation

I am becoming my best self.
My business reflects my commitment to excellence.
Referrals are flowing from my commitment to
exceptional service.

My S.M.A.R.T. Goals for the Week Beginning:

Specific	Measurable	Actionable	Relevant	Time-bound
This week I will: *<< insert goal >>*	I know that this goal has been accomplished when: *<insert description>*	I must take the following actions to make this goal a reality: 1. 2. 3.	Accomplishing this goal brings me closer to my vision of: *<insert short description of your vision>*	I will accomplish this goal by: *<insert day, date and time.>* *This date should be within the next 7 days.

LESSON 52

HONOR YOUR MESSAGE

*This is the Message I've been set apart to proclaim as
preacher, emissary, and teacher.
It's also the cause of all this trouble I'm in.
But I have no regrets.*

*I couldn't be more sure of my ground -
the One I've trusted in can take care of what he's trusted me
to do right to the end.*

2 Timothy 1:11 (The Message)

Building a legacy business that will serve the world beyond
your natural life is not easy. This Work not only requires
integrity, but also a refusal to be deceitful, misuse others or
otherwise engage in unethical business practices.

It may feel that operating a business built on Christian
principles makes things harder. Do not give in to this feeling.
Instead, trust that your commitment to doing what is right will
pay big dividends in the long run.

Here's why ....

Your business becomes a messenger for God when you are
faithful, diligent and bold in doing your Work while praising
God throughout your journey of Christianpreneurship. This
message that your business is shouting out to the world says,
"all things are possible through Jesus Christ."

The fruits of your labor are also messengers for God. These messengers are shouting out to Christianpreneurs - "your gifts will make room for you, lead you into greatness and serve the world in the process."

The business born from the vision God has given you is the Work God has entrusted to you. Don't betray God's trust.

Create products that transform how people think.
Develop systems that make things more effective.
Offer services that alleviate pain.
Provide advice that helps people avoid liability.

Do the Work that you know has been entrusted to you. Then, have faith that God will take care of you along your journey to blessings that have been ordained for your life. This is the path to living with no regrets.

Dear Lord,

I give you all honor, glory and praise for blessing me with life and the desire to build a business that serves you. Please help me build a business that honors you and leads people to Christ. As I look forward to a new week, I also ask...

Thank you for entrusting me with your Work.

_____   _____
Name   *Date*

Lesson 52 Affirmation

My revenue reflects my commitment to excellence and my diligence in doing the Work that God has entrusted to me.

My S.M.A.R.T. Goals for the Week Beginning:

SPECIFIC	**M**EASURABLE	**A**CTIONABLE	**R**ELEVANT	**T**IME-BOUND
This week I will: *<< insert goal >>*	I know that this goal has been accomplished when: *<insert description>*	I must take the following actions to make this goal a reality: 1. 2. 3.	Accomplishing this goal brings me closer to my vision of: *<insert short description of your vision>*	I will accomplish this goal by: *<insert day, date and time.>* *This date should be within the next 7 days.

222

For your convenience, below is a larger version of
the **S.M.A.R.T.** Goals Chart.

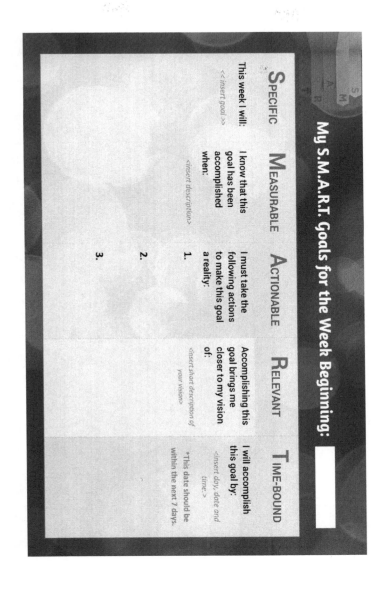

My S.M.A.R.T. Goals for the Week Beginning:

SPECIFIC	MEASURABLE	ACTIONABLE	RELEVANT	TIME-BOUND
This week I will:	I know that this goal has been accomplished when:	I must take the following actions to make this goal a reality:	Accomplishing this goal brings me closer to my vision of:	I will accomplish this goal by:
<< insert goal >>	<insert description>	1.	<insert short description of your vision>	<insert day, date and time>
		2.		*This date should be within the next 7 days.
		3.		

APPENDIX

APPENDIX

ACKNOWLEDGEMENTS

To my Lord and Savior, Jesus Christ, thank you for entrusting me with this Work of sharing your message with people around the world.

To my church family at Greater St. Mark A.M.E. Church in Hemingway, SC - I say thank you. Your love, support, guidance and discipline have molded me into the woman I am today. I learned so while growing up in church as a Girl Scout, YPD leader, Sunday School Secretary and Church Musician thanks to your care.

To my church family at Alfred Street Baptist Church in Alexandra, VA, where Rev. Dr. Howard-John Wesley is the senior pastor, and especially my Discipleship Group #22 – thank you for all of your love, encouragement and prayers.

Thank you Rev. Dr. David D. Ireland, founder and lead pastor of Christ Church in Rockaway and Montclair, NJ. Your sermons about the business and wealth building acumen of Job have transformed my life.

ACKNOWLEDGEMENTS

Thank you Dr. Will Moreland, S.W. (Sha') Cannon, Allison Cain and Tina R. Mills for your support and encouragement in writing two books of substance in two months! Y'all have become my family and I appreciate each of you more than words can express.

Thank you to my brothers Monty and Duane Cooper, sis-in-love – Angeleen Cooper, uncles, aunts, cousins and friends for believing in me, supporting me, sharing this book with others on Facebook and Twitter (I see you! xo) and forgiving me when I'm not always able to be physically present at gatherings. Please know that I am always there in spirit.

Thank you to my Busboys and Poets family at 5th and K. I appreciate you for letting me hang out with you at the community table while I wrote and edited much of this book. Thanks for remembering my favorite latte and for your words of encouragement throughout the process of bringing this Work to life. I appreciate you!

ACTIONeers!

Thanks for being a part of my Periscope family. I love and appreciate you for your time, your hearts, your feedback, your encouragement and most importantly, your prayers.

Special shout outs to:

Annalisa Sharp Babich
Cee Cee H. Caldwell-Miller
Dawn Fitch
Dr. Aikyna Finch
Dr. Nicola Brown
Dr. Stacie NC Grant
Dawn E. Stephens
Jacqueline Ebanks
Jesse Bryant
Keith Shepard
Victoria Sandoval
LaMeel Kimse
Lesley F. McClendon
Lynette Martin
Nolan McClinton
Patricia Bias Morrison
Reginald Watkins
Sharon Addison
Tanya Blue
Greg "The Big Dreamer" Walker

Brooke-Sidney J. Harbour
Decoda Roberts
Devon Clark
Dr. Dwanda Farmer
Dr. Rosche
Dr. Zoe Fludd
Felicia Bentine Padilla
Jason Hodge
Karen Y. Kirkland
Kim Bogard
Kevin Farris
L. Denise Jackson
Linda Hillman
Madalyn M. Richardson
Patrick Dewayne Stewart
Pastor Perry Coates
Shannon Griffin
Susan Fish
Tora Spraggs
Zakia Ringgold

Linked**in**. Profile and Company Page Consulting

WE WILL REVIEW AND OPTIMIZE YOUR EXISTING LINKEDIN
PROFILE AND COMPANY PAGE OR CREATE THESE PAGES FOR YOU
IF YOU DO NOT ALREADY HAVE THEM.

This package includes:

1 Development and delivery of a keyword optimized profile and company/firm description to significantly increase the placement of your pages in LinkedIn searches;

2 Specific recommendations for the LinkedIn groups you should join (based on your business objectives) and exactly what to do when you join and

3 30-day plan for action for leveraging the power of LinkedIn to have more profitable conversations. No resume, no problem. We'll work with you to develop the content that you need for your LinkedIn pages.

Contact Us:

Email: WeCare@UpwardAction.com

Skype: TC Cooper @ UpwardAction

Telephone: (800) 753-6576

Website: www.UpwardAction.com

A PROFITABLE SOCIAL ADVERTISING CAMPAIGN STARTS WITH A TARGETED SOCIAL MEDIA STRATEGY.

At UpwardAction®, our social media marketing services are designed to help our clients attract their ideal clients. Work with us and we'll provide you with a customized plan that is unique to your business and your industry.

When you are ready for results, we're ready to talk.

- Social Media Consultation
- Social Media Advertising Implementation
- Social Media Content Development

Contact Us:

Email:	WeCare@UpwardAction.com
Skype:	TC Cooper @ UpwardAction
Telephone:	(800) 753-6576
Website:	www.UpwardAction.com

I have had the great pleasure of bringing TC in for entrepreneur training programs. As someone who has taught entrepreneurship for many years and brought in countless speakers and business coaches, I can say without hesitation that Tasha Cooper is the best speaker and business coach that I have ever seen. She is a brilliant business strategist who also has outstanding communication skills. You literally cannot even write down all the great business solutions that she produces! I fully recommend Tasha with my highest praise. **John Childress,** *Levin Institute FastTrac Program*

TC, thank you very much for your time and energy in presenting the three Build Momentum with Social Media sessions for our members. The feedback from the lawyers was very positive. It was especially helpful that you were able to demonstrate how a lawyer can turn her/his LinkedIn profile into a dynamic tool for building a network and communicating one's problem solving ability and expertise. Showing lawyers how and when to use Twitter was very useful because you provided a clear strategy for getting results from this tool. **Daniel Mills,** *The District of Columbia Bar*

ABOUT THE AUTHOR

Tasha (TC) Cooper is a Christianpreneur, attorney and professional speaker. She also serves in the position of president of UpwardAction® LLC - a social marketing and online publishing agency. TC has been featured in magazines that include Black Enterprise, inBIZ and the California Bar Journal. She is also the author of LinkedIn for Lawyerprenurs: Strategies to Increase Your Impact, Influence and Income.

TC is committed to leveraging the power of the Internet to help Christianpreneurs all over the globe increase their impact, influence and ultimately income. She does this by building online platforms that serve people around the world though email newsletters, digital programs and online communities.

At UpwardAction®, TC has not only guided law firms, small business owners, nonprofit organizations and state associations – she has had the privilege of launching several web portals with programming designed to empower people and help them do the Work they have been called to do.

TC is a proud graduate of Hampton University (Hampton, VA) and Columbia Law School (New York, NY), where she was a Harlan Fiske Stone Scholar. She has also completed executive coach training at Coach University. TC resides in Washington, DC – one of her two favorite cities in the world.